PRAISE FOR
YOU'RE THE PROBLEM (AND THE SOLUTION)

"This book is full of the wisdom and practical guidance that Bob Clements is known for through his popular workshops for dealership owners and managers. The seven habits that Bob and his co-author Sara Hey have identified will help dealers improve their financial management practices, identify successful growth strategies, and motivate employees. Bob and Sara understand what makes successful dealerships tick . . . and they've shared it all in this book."

PHIL INGRASSIA, President, RVDA

"Bob and Sara have produced a guide for equipment dealers of all sizes and types. Success is nearly a certainty by placing their plan into action. The seven habits detailed in this fantastic reference guide are not only good for business but for life. This book is a must read!"

KIM ROMINGER, President/CEO, Equipment Dealers Association

"I loved this book. As a professional with more than twenty-five years working with dealers as a corporate executive and owning my own business, I said "exactly" and "right-on" many times while reading. BCI knows and values dealers. The practical, right-sized and specific examples are easy to follow. More importantly, the tools and ideas are right there and ready for you to implement. I recommend this book for existing dealers, new dealers, and for key employees at dealerships."

PAIGE WITTMAN, Co-Owner, Miller Wittman Retail Design Group

"Sara Hey and Bob Clements have written a must-read guide to running a dealership. Learn from the best as they take you through common sense approaches to creating a vision, equipping your people and managing departments. They use real-life stories to explain the seven overarching habits of being a successful dealership, PLUS they give you proven management formulas for parts, service, and sales."

WARREN S. SELLERS, Sellers Expositions

"Helping dealers define and achieve their goals has been a lifelong passion for Bob and Sara and that certainly comes through clearly in the pages of *You're the Problem (and the Solution)*. The seven habits they define are foundational to success in a challenging industry and regardless of where you are in your journey as a dealer, you'll find something here to take you to the next level."

MICHAEL ELLIS, Publisher, Lessiter Media – Rural Lifestyle Dealer

"As a manufacturer of products sold through a dealer network, we've relied on the experience and expertise of Bob Clements and Sara Hey at Bob Clements International to help our dealers and our business grow. They take the time to listen and are passionate about the success of dealers and manufacturers. That knowledge and enthusiasm is showcased perfectly in this book."

MIKE DRAPER, Sales & Marketing Manager, Voyager Industries (manufacturer of Bear Track Trailers)

"We engaged Bob a decade ago when our service department was trending in the wrong direction. His expertise provided scaffolding for the growth we've seen since then, and his operating systems are the foundation of our processes today. I firmly believe that you can learn everything about a dealership by observing the operations of the service department, and there is no sustainable or profitable growth without excellence in this function. Without exaggeration, Bob changed the course of my dealership."

SPENCER COLEMAN, Dealer Principle

"We have been a BCI customer for close to two decades. We proudly recommend their services. If you are in need of no-nonsense, tactical, insightful business guidance and assistance, there is no one better. This book is an extension of this wonderful combination, that includes storytelling and a sense of humor, that makes the learning process enjoyable."

RICK BRYAN, CEO, Bryan Equipment Sales, Inc.

"Pick up this book and take control of your dealership!! As a former dealership Service Manager this book is a great insight into the issues we all face and how we can tackle them. Written with some light hearted lines it hit home with me on many relatable subjects. One to keep on the shelf as you will always be reaching for it!!!"

MARTIN TYLER, Business Development Manager - Service, Kubota (UK) Ltd

"Bob and the team are an amazing contributor to the OPE industry and the title of this book sums up their approach to the issues and possibilities surrounding today's dealers."

DUNCAN MURRAY-CLARKE, Owner *Service Dealer* Magazine (UK), *Turf Pro* (UK), Garden Trader (UK) and My Mower Specialist (USA)

YOU'RE THE PROBLEM

AND THE SOLUTION!

Proven Habits to Reclaim Your Sanity, Your Life, and Your Dealership

BOB CLEMENTS & SARA HEY

Be the Solution!
Sara Hey -
Bob Clements

StoryTell
Published by StoryTell, LLC
2335 North Lincoln Ave Chicago, IL 60614, USA

First Printing, October 2020
Copyright © 2020 by Bob Clements International, Sara Hey, and Bob Clements

Printed in the United States of America

While the author has made every effort to provide accurate telephone numbers, Internet addresses, and other contact information at the time of publication, neither the publisher nor the author assumes any responsibility for errors or for changes that occur after publication. Further, publisher does not have any control over and does not assume any responsibility for the author or third-party websites or their content.

Disclaimer of Consultation Relationship/Disclaimer of Guarantee of Future Results
The information presented on the BCI website or affiliated website, at any BCI events or programs, and any of the materials, videos or specific modules presented have been provided for informational purposes only. It does not constitute advice specifically for your business. The receipt of this information does not establish a consultation relationship. Proper advice can only be given upon consideration of all relevant facts and laws specific to your situation. The exact nature of your situation will depend on many facts not known to us at this time. You should understand that the advice and information contained at this event, in our materials, on a BCI or BCI affiliates website or links to and from this website are general and that your own situation may vary. Any results set forth herein are based upon the facts of that particular situation and do not represent a promise or guarantee of future results. Every situation is different and must be judged on its own merits. No guarantees are represented by the information presented in, on or as a result of this event. [Note: Some of the materials, examples, pictures or videos featured herein may be simulations.]

Table of Contents

Introduction

I work in a family business, but this is not just any family business. This is a business that my mom and dad started, my mom currently runs, bears my dad's name (because we don't want him to forget his name as he gets older), and currently employs all three kids and my sister-in-law. To say, "the gang's all here" would be an understatement. In addition to our biological family, the other people who make up the team at Bob Clements International (BCI for short) are people who have become like family. We work together, have fun together, and are all passionate about achieving our mission: to help dealers achieve success. We are all here, and all in each other's business, both literally and figuratively. The other thing that's unique about our business is that we work with thousands of other businesses, specifically dealerships, who are in the same situation as us.

When my mom and dad started BCI, I don't think they had any idea of the effect they would have on dealerships around the world. Growing up (and providing child labor for our family business), I never understood the impact of what they were doing. But, when it came down to it, they were providing hope to dealers around the world. Hope that showed the owners and managers of these dealerships that they were doing work that mattered; hope that there was a future for them; and hope that, one day, when they retired from the business it could and would go on. They built a business that was founded on providing hope, rooted in hard work, and established on best practices and processes.

Now, as I've moved past the child-labor phase of the family business, I have come to realize that what they created is not for a specific dealer industry, but it is for all dealership owners and managers. It is for the dealership who is considering closing their doors because they are just tired and have no fight left. It's for the owner who is putting all of their retirement savings back into the dealership just to keep the business afloat. It's for the owners who wonder if they will ever be able to sell their business or pass it on to the next generation. What my mom and dad have built through BCI is for every dealership owner who has ever wondered why they continue to do this day after day, and for those who are ready to take control of their business instead of letting their business control them. And that shift, that moment, when a dealer decides they are sick of the status quo, is where change and hope collide.

Over the years that I have been involved in the dealership world, I discovered something. I found that some dealers were in a never-ending, all-consuming stream of struggle, day after day, while others seemed to be successful regardless of what happened to them or their dealership. It made me wonder, what separated the thousands of successful dealers we have worked with from the ones that could never get ahead? It came down to habits. Most of the dealers we highlight in this book wouldn't call what has made them to not only survive, but succeed, habits. They might call it focus, perseverance, or hard work. But what it comes down to is this: these dealers have worked with a singular focus, and their "hard work" has become part of their DNA, something they do naturally, day in and day out, without thinking. And in my mind, that's a habit.

About a year ago, our entire BCI team decided that we wanted to understand this further so we could help all dealers who were willing to put in the work necessary to reclaim their sanity, life, and dealership. So, that's what we did. We spent time every Monday morning for almost a year, meeting as a team and talking about specific dealers that were successful and what they had in common.

As our team dug further into what separated the dealers who were in a never-ending cycle of survival from the ones who were truly winning, we began to see that there were seven overarching habits consistent among the best of the best. It all made sense; these were what separated the dealers who were successful from the ones who were stuck on a perpetual bumper car ride, never going anywhere and still ending up with minor whiplash.

Over the year, as we identified the habits, we took it one step further and interviewed the dealers who exhibited these habits, and what we found is detailed for you in this book. Each of these habits is accompanied by stories of dealers who are successful and live and breathe the habits outlined.

Perhaps you want to reach a new level of success in your business. You might be asking yourself, "Where do I start? Is it even possible?" The answer is yes; it is possible! It begins with you simply deciding to start the process of transformation and put in the work to develop the habits outlined in this book.

Good habits aren't created by accident. They take intentionality and work, but once you create a strong habit, it creates momentum for the next one. You have already taken the first step toward change by walking through this book with us. We are here cheering you on and can't wait to see how you take these habits, apply them to your dealership, and experience the results you have always dreamed of.

HOW DO WE DEFINE SUCCESS?

There is no one-size-fits-all definition of success. When we asked our dealers what success looked like to them, there was a wide range of responses. You see, success simply looks different for everyone.

Have you ever looked at other people or businesses and assumed they are successful only to find out later that your assumption was 100 percent wrong? The truth is that you and I have a very limited perspective of what happens behind the scenes. We think, *Wow, they must be killing it! Look at their house, their vehicles, their building, their inventory.* When in fact they may be barely surviving and struggling just to keep their doors open. What is not uncommon to find is that often the people who look the most successful are many times the ones who are struggling the most.

So, what is your definition of success? Is it defined by money, peace of mind, a quality of life, acquisitions, or family? How would you finish the sentence: "I would be achieving success if
_____?"

It might be a combination of the items listed above, or perhaps a more short-term goal, like simply getting caught up on your past-due bills, taxes, or debt. As you wrestle with defining what success looks like to you, keep in mind the realities about success.

Your Understanding of Success Can Change Over Time

Think back ten years. Think about who you were and where you were in life. Really think about yourself. It's okay, I'll wait. First, where were you living and what was in your closet? What type of vehicle were you driving? Who were the people in your circle of friends and family at that time? What did you do outside of your business? Were you even in your dealership ten years ago? Take a minute and think about who you were ten years ago. Now that you are there, what was your idea of success then?

Maybe ten years ago success was adding a new line of products at your dealership, or to be profitable enough to give out Christmas bonuses (or take one for yourself), or to purchase your first vehicle or first home, or to add a second location, or to get your kids through high school or college. Has your definition of success from ten years ago changed? My guess is probably yes.

As you grow and develop as an individual, your personal view of what it means to achieve success also changes and adapts. You don't just attain success and in one moment, magically achieve everything you had set out to do in your life. You may know people who have attained success in high school and college and never moved past that short-lived achievement. But people who are successful don't view success as a stagnant goal to attain. As successful people grow, learn, and develop, so does their understanding and definition of success.

Your Definition of Success Looks Different from Anyone Else's

Your definition of success will be different than the next person's; it is unique to you. Your manufacturers can't dictate what success looks like to you, the person at your church can't tell you what success should look like, and there is no way your employees can decide if you have achieved success or not. A true understanding of success is a personal thing; it's like when you were a child and you were asked what you wanted to be when you grew up. Everyone wanted to be something different and none of them were wrong, unless you wanted to be something other than a dolphin trainer (yes, that is what I wanted to be!).

Could you imagine a world where everyone was striving to become and achieve the exact same thing? What would the world be like if the only thing that represented success was being a famous musician or lawyer or working in retail sales? Could you imagine what our society would lack if we all had the exact same idea of success?

While it might seem like the easy thing to do, to take on and adapt to someone else's idea of success for your life, you have to fight this with everything in you, to not live your life and run your business by the standards set by other people.

Why? Because your definition of success is needed in this world! The moment you start working toward someone else's version of success, you immediately become an impostor. You aren't true to yourself. You aren't true to your business. You aren't true to your people. Your definition of success is the right one . . . for you. It is relevant, needed, and worthy. Define it and own it.

One thing, however, that is fundamental to the success of any dealership is profitability. In a dealership, for you to keep your doors open you must be profitable. If not, you would be better off to spend your time, and would likely make more money, working at the local fast-food restaurant down the street. Regardless of what your version of success looks like, profitability is an over-arching goal of your business. So, walk along with us as we share how the dealers we work with have developed habits in their business and life that are helping them reclaim their sanity, their life, and their dealerships.

HABIT ONE:

Develop a Clear Vision for the Future

I'M THE PROBLEM: *I'm just winging it.*
I'M THE SOLUTION: *I have clear direction.*

Sara and I had just finished our last program for the morning at the GIE+EXPO in Louisville, Kentucky. As I walked off the stage, a couple, who had attended my program, caught my attention. They were in their mid-forties, standing next to the wall, dressed in matching polo shirts with their dealership logo brightly proclaiming their names. I could see them trying to decide if they should talk with me, so I walked up, extended my hand, and thanked them for attending my workshop.

After they introduced themselves as Ron and Marsha, Ron looked at his wife and said, "Go ahead and ask him." "Ask me what?" I said. At that moment, the floodgate of questions started. We talked about everything from what to do about a service technician who was holding them hostage, to how to motivate and compensate employees. We talked about how to increase profits in their parts department and how they could get to the point of ever getting away from the dealership and have a life. We discussed the number of product lines they were carrying and if I thought they would ever be able to sell their dealership in the future.

Over that next hour I would learn about their business, their struggles, and the desperation they were feeling. As I asked questions about their employees, each of their departments, and their financial situation, both for the business and personally, it was apparent that they were on the verge of burnout. They were working more hours than they should, they were not taking out the money the business should have been providing for them, and two of their ten employees were not even close to producing the work they should based upon how much they were each being paid. Their business had taken over their lives. It was running them into the ground, and they had no idea how to stop it.

While there were a multitude of issues to deal with, the most important way I could help them, in the short amount of time we had, was to get them re-focused. I needed them to go back to the beginning and remember why they started their business in the first place. I needed them to remember the dream, what they had hoped to achieve, and why it was important to them. I needed them to take whatever small spark of passion they had left and rekindle it, so it could guide them as they moved forward in dealing with their people, their vendors, the bankers, and themselves.

Ron and Marsha were not unlike many others running dealerships and small businesses. They were working themselves into the ground because they had lost track of why they started the business in the beginning; they had lost their vision. Vison is a powerful and important part of a dealership. A well-defined vision gives you direction, helps you make decisions, and encourages you when there seems to be little to be encouraged by. It is like a fire in the dark of night that pushes away the darkness and gives you comfort and hope. But, like a fire, it has to be built and tended to. Once your vision is established, you must continually feed it fuel to keep it bright and burning. Vision at its core is fueled by dreams and conversations.

At one time, this couple had a vision for their dealership. But, over the years, they had allowed circumstances and the daily grind of the business and life to pull their eyes off their focus. While the fire was not completely out, it was burning on embers; the vision they had was starving for fuel.

So, we started with a conversation. I asked them to tell me about the time they made the decision to open the dealership. Within minutes, I could see them both starting to gain some of their excitement back. I challenged them to sit down over lunch and relive the day they decided to open the dealership. I asked them to write down their thoughts and feelings. You see, they needed to refuel their vision, based upon where they were today, and to begin the process of setting goals. These goals were critical to restarting the journey toward reaching and achieving the dreams they once had.

As you think about your dealership, the vision and goals you have, understand that they will have an impact not only on you but on your people as well. In our company, our entire team regularly reviews our mission statement and five-year vision. We work together setting and achieving the goals necessary to attain that vision. Communicating a clear vision for your dealership and working with your employees to set achievable goals will go a long way in improved performance for everyone in your business.

Later that afternoon, I had an opportunity to sit down again with Ron and Marsha to help them clarify and refine their mission statement, their core values, and the vision for the next few years.

For both Ron and Marsha, this one afternoon changed the direction of their dealership and their future. Let's join Sara as she shows you how to establish your mission, core values, and vision, the first and most important steps toward achieving success in your business.

• • •

I have often said, an owner has three main responsibilities in a dealership or business of any type. For most owners, the idea of only having three responsibilities sounds like a vacation complete with a beach, a drink, and a book. Now, these aren't inclusive of everything that most of you have to do, but, in my opinion, these are the three most important things. As the owner . . .

1. You are responsible for casting a vision for the dealership. This answers the question "Where are we going?"
2. You are responsible for developing a strategy. This answers the question, "How are we going to accomplish the vision?"
3. You are responsible for developing your people. This answers the question "Who do I need to get there?"

As an owner, you will never be able to reach a new level of success without making these three tasks your primary job focus. Without a vision, you have nothing to aim for and there is no clear purpose behind all you are doing. Without a strategy, your vision does not have legs to stand on. It is simply a wish and a dream. And without getting your people on board and working to develop them, you are running against the wind in a never-ending vacuum tube. Sounds terrible, doesn't it?

So, are you ready to implement the number one habit of all successful dealers and become the solution and not the problem? Are you ready to experience what it feels like to win and be successful? Then, let's get started.

It's all about that base. You must build a solid foundation. (If you are still having doubts, don't skip this section!)

For some of you, I feel the eye rolls and the hesitation that is probably in your mind right now. You are saying, "Sara, I'm just trying to make payroll. Why does this really matter? I thought this book was going to fix my dealership." For you, as for many dealers, this will be the first step in regaining control and achieving success in your dealership. I promise, we will outline steps you can take to make significant improvement in profitability, processes, and people. But for now, believe me, this is important.

Have you ever built something? A house, a garage, a Christmas present for your kid on Christmas Eve that took way more time than you thought? Cool, me neither. Whether it's a dealership or a building, there is nothing more important than the foundation it is set upon. That base will ultimately determine how long it will stand, and the amount of stress it can handle. Building a successful dealership with a weak and flawed foundation will never bring you the success you want. Cracks will begin to develop during times of stress, just like a house that is built on a bad foundation. The doors will stick, the floors will creak, and no number of small fixes or trips to the hardware store will ever make it right.

It is the foundation that allows you to create a solid, stable platform that you, your employees, and your family members can build from. Good, solid employees will not stay in a dealership that has a weak and crumbling foundation. You have worked tirelessly and invested a lot of money to find and keep good technicians, parts people, salespeople, and other support people for your dealership. If you want to keep them, you must provide a solid foundation of clarity. Never forget that your people are the heartbeat of your business. For many of you, your people are why you do what you do. And a lack of clarity for your people is a recipe for disaster.

Beyond that, as new generations of employees and customers walk through your doors, they expect you to stand for something. For anything. We live in a world that just wants you to take a stand. "Please," they are saying, "let us know what you're about." Ironically, because we have so many mixed messages in the world today, a lack of a mission, core values, and vision only adds to the noise. I want your mission, core values, and vision to become the drumbeat that your people march to. I want it to become the rallying cry, the uniting force, that no matter what happens within the walls of your dealership, your people and customers can always rely on one thing—as the leader, you know who you are and where you are going.

It sounds simple, doesn't it? But you and I both know just because something is simple doesn't mean it's easy. The art of discovering your purpose, whether personally or in business, is often a complex and challenging process. We are all drawn to something that we can find purpose in, and the same is true for your people and your dealership.

MISSION
(WHAT'S YOUR PURPOSE?)

Your mission, or purpose, is what will always be true about you. The mission of your dealership won't change over time. When my parents started our company in the '80s, they had the same mission (but different hairstyles) that we do today. Both now and then, our mission is to *"Help Dealers Achieve Success."* Was it articulated and written down at that point? Probably not; however, it has always been the purpose of our company.

My guess is that you, as an owner or manager, have a pretty good idea of what the mission of your dealership is. Maybe you haven't actually put it into words or been very effective in communicating your mission, but it's there and it's always been the same. It is the reason you went into business. It is what you want to be known for, and it is what keeps you motivated to face another day.

Bob continued to work with that couple from Louisville through one of BCI's dealer programs, and soon after, they had reestablished their mission. As they took time and gave themselves space to remember why they started their business, it was crystal clear to them. They wanted to make a positive impact on their community, one customer at a time. Up to that moment, would they have been able to identify that as their mission? Probably not, but it had been true from day one and was why they continued running their dealership today. Because they took the time to remember why they started their dealership in the first place, they were able to begin to make forward progress again, working toward something, and they were able to communicate it to their employees and their customers. It was a great beginning.

My guess is that you, as an owner or manager, know what your mission is or why you exist, but you just haven't been very clear in communicating it to your employees or yourself. Do you need to rediscover your mission? Ask yourself, what will always be true about your dealership?

The mission of your dealership doesn't have to be an earth-shattering declaration. Maybe it's that you provide a needed service for the community, or you treat every customer with dignity and hope they leave a little better because they interacted with you and your people. Maybe your mission is focused on providing good lives for your family and the families of your employees. Maybe, just maybe, you're not sure. You feel like you have been doing this for so long, and the idea of a mission or purpose for what you are doing sounds a little scary. So, let's keep it simple.

Try this: Go out to a park or coffee shop or even just to your truck, anywhere you can be by yourself and think. Shoot, if you need to go to the bathroom and lock the door, then do that. Taking this time is something you need to do. The health of your dealership is dependent on this. If there is someone who has been along with you on this journey from the start, bring them with you. (Well, not to the bathroom, that's just awkward.) Just like Ron and Marsha at the GIE+EXPO, take a piece of paper and jot down your thoughts. Ask yourself questions like: In regard to the business, what is most important to me? Who is most important to me? What do I want to be known for? What do I want the business to be known for? If I could only focus on one thing and do it well, what would that be? Very soon, you will start to see what is most important to you as a business owner.

Take what you have and narrow it down to a short statement—seven to ten words is a good target. It should be able to fit on a T-shirt, billboard, or sign in your dealership. Then, once you have it, let it sit for a few days. As you think about it, see if it continues to represent who you are and what you want to be. Share it with a friend or an advisor and ask them to tell you what they really think, with no filter.

Having a clear mission will help you retain good people. All people want to be apart of something that matters and that makes a difference, so make it a priority to communicate your mission to your team, clearly and regularly.

It is often said that in marketing a customer must see, hear, or experience a message seven times before they make a buying decision. What if we took the same stance with our employees? What if we assumed that we were going to have to communicate our mission (and core values and vision) seven different ways before they understood it, remembered it, believed it? Your people need to know what a win looks like in your dealership. It's not uncommon for a dealer to say to Bob or myself, "I feel like I have told this technician what I expect of them five times already." We would both respond the same way: "Way to go! Only two more times left."

When we understand that we have flaws in communication, it allows us to find ways to think differently about getting people on board with what we are trying to do, where we are trying to go, and how we are trying to do it.

Think about taking this a step further and creating mission statements for each department in your dealership, so, again, your people know what their specific purpose is in their department. For example, here are some departmental mission statements from four dealers we work with.

> *Service Department:* To bring every product back to
> OEM specifications
> *Parts Department:* To maintain 90 percent of the parts
> that counter customers and our service department
> need when they need them
> *Sales Department:* Pair every customer with the right
> piece of equipment
> *Rental Department:* To have the units customers need in
> excellent condition

Regardless of other goals, the mission is set, and the objective established.

At the end of the day, establishing a mission statement tells the world why you exist. It affects how you make decisions. It affects how you treat people. It affects everything you do. Dealers who consistently achieve success understand that in order to create a business that will survive long past themselves, a clear mission is a cornerstone and that communicating it over and over is essential.

CORE VALUES
(HOW DO YOU DO BUSINESS?)

Your core values, in their simplest form, explain how you want business done.

The ultimate reason we establish core values is threefold:

1. Your customers expect a consistent experience.

Today, the customer experience is everything. That hasn't always been the case. Customers have gone from a place of "save me money" (where the experience didn't matter as much), to "save me time," where the most important factor in their decision to work with you is related to their experience.

Each time your customer interacts with you, your people, and your dealership, they expect to have a consistent experience. Think about the last time you went through a drive-through. Other than wondering why in the world you ordered the large fries, the experience was probably mediocre. (Unless you went to Chick-fil-A, and it was their pleasure to serve you. We see you, Chick-fil-A.) Regardless of where you choose to get your meal stuffed out a window in under three minutes, you always know what to expect. Your customers need the same thing from your dealership.

It's up to you to identify the expectations of your customers and meet or exceed those expectations. The way you make this happen, regardless of who in your dealership is interacting with the customer, is through a strong set of core values in combination with your mission and vision statements. The combination of these three things will allow any customer who interacts with your dealership to be treated as if you were working with them yourself.

2. You want employees to conduct themselves inside your business exactly as you would.

If you could clone yourself, would you? This is a question that has been around for as long as sliced bread, which I assume has been around forever. The idea of cloning yourself, especially to most entrepreneurs, sounds like an incredible opportunity. Just think about everything you could get done in a day if there were ten more of you running around.

Do we want our employees to think in the same way we do? Yes, and no. Now, I know that sounds as non-committal as a politician's answer, and it is. But hear me out. Yes, we want them to think about working with a customer in the same way, but no we don't because we want them to bring their own ideas and skills to the situation.

Where is the easy button that allows you to simultaneously have your employees think and react like you would? You guessed it. Your core values. Core values give you the power to put up a fence around your people. It allows you to say, "As long as you make your decisions with these three to five things in mind, no matter what decision you make, there will not be any repercussions. If you step out of the boundary of these core values, that's where problems begin."

Let me give you an example. When I was growing up, I spent a lot of time on my grandparents' farm in a small town called Barnard, Missouri. Around the farm was an electric fence, used to keep the cows, and grandkids, in. Was the electric fence ever on? Honestly, I have no idea, but my guess is probably not. But my brother, sister, and I knew we had free reign of all our grandparents' land, as long as we stayed inside the fence.

This is all you are trying to do with core values. Empower your

"Do more for the customer than they expect." New customers to Dale's gas station were stunned that the front of their car was vacuumed as they were getting fuel.

"Always be honest in what you say and do." Again, Bob would tell you that his grandfather, Dale, was all about honesty. Whether the customer wanted to hear it or not, Dale always shot straight with them.

His vision was focused, *to be better than the competition*, which in his case just happened to be right across the street selling gas for the exact same price that Dale was selling his for. Bob's granddad knew the only thing he had to set his station apart from his competitors were the people who worked for him. And according to Bob, he worked tirelessly to keep all his people focused on those three key elements. Whether Dale was at the station or at home putting up hay while his people ran the station, he knew he had given his team the ability to make like-minded decisions without him being there.

This set of decision-making references is also helpful when a "once in a lifetime" opportunity comes up. You know the ones I'm talking about. "Should I add a partner?" (No. No. No. No.) "I have an opportunity to open another location, does this make sense?" (Probably not, this is your ego talking.) "My kids just graduated, should they join the business?" (Only if they have a skill you need, and you have an opening.) You simply need to ask the question, "Does it match our mission, vision, and core values?" If yes, do it. Go all in. If no, respect the boundaries you have put in place to help you succeed.

VISION
(WHAT ARE YOU AIMING FOR?)

If your company's mission describes what you are all about and your core values define how you operate your business, then your vision will communicate what you are aiming for as a dealership.

When thinking about establishing your vision, it's important to keep in mind that your vision should be motivational, challenging, and future focused.

During our live events, Bob often tells the story about how the United States put the first man on the moon. He reminds the group of the struggles the US encountered in the beginning of the space program, how the (former) Soviet Union had made great strides in their rocket development, and how the US was falling behind. As he tells it, there was a turning point when former President John Kennedy gave the famous "Moon Shot" speech in 1961. As Bob points out, the US didn't have the technology, they didn't have adequately trained people, and they were behind in every aspect of the space race. Despite all of that, because of a leader who had the ability to cast a powerful vision for the country, eight years later two United States astronauts were the first people to ever step foot on the moon and return safely back to earth. Bob explained to the owners and managers that the vision President Kennedy cast for the country had the most important elements that all visions must include. His vision *motivated* the country to strive to achieve something seemingly impossible. President Kennedy *challenged* the country to achieve the goal before the end of the decade—we landed in 1969. And the vision was *future focused*—we would never be the same country again if we could achieve this incredible task. So, let's look at how you can incorporate all three of these components into your vision statement.

Motivational — You want to create a vision that your people will be excited about. What's something that would light your soul on fire and that you feel your people would be fired up about?

Challenging — This vision should not be something that can be accomplished in the next week, month, or year. This is a major challenge that might seem impossible to achieve at this moment. I want to encourage you to think big! And, whatever you think is big, go bigger! You will be surprised at what you can achieve when everyone is on board and moving in the same direction. The number of times we have had dealers achieve their vision, in half the time, is mind-blowing. So, go big!

Future-focused — Your vision should be cast over a five-year period, at minimum, for most dealerships. This is the big goal we are moving toward every single day.

We have several dealerships that have created for themselves a "Debt-free dealership in five years." Listen, this is a huge, almost insurmountable vision for a dealership. They all have aired the same concerns. *What if I lose people over this? What if we don't achieve it? What if . . . ?*

I understand the nerves about this. Any change can be significant, but what happens if you just continue business as usual? What if, ten years from now, you find yourself in exactly the same place you are today? What if nothing changes? That should incite more fear in you than if you are going to lose someone who doesn't buy into what you were doing in the first place.

One dealer we work with had established a long-term vision for their dealership that involved hitting specific sales numbers each year. It was the last week of the second year, and they were about $20,000 short of the goal. Every employee pulled together. The service department pushed to finish a couple of big jobs that got closed. The service manager scrambled to get all warranties filed. The parts department got their returns processed and the sales-people followed up on every quote that could possibly close by the end of the year. As a team, focused on the goal, they exceeded their number by over $4,000. It was an exciting moment for the dealership and their entire team.

Does your mission, core values, and vision matter if you have a small team? YES!

The number one thing we see as an indicator for success in a dealership, regardless of what success looks like for you, is that you know why you exist, where you are going, and what your plan is to get there. That's it. Mic drop. We could finish this book now and we would have communicated the most important thing, but trust me that's not going to happen. We still have so much we want to say. Hard to believe, I know.

We work with every size dealership you can imagine from very small to very large, multi-location groups. And whether a dealer has a small team or a large number of employees, we have seen positive results when you have in place the winning trifecta, as I like to call it. Those who have taken time to define these three guiding principles are able to find and retain people in a much more efficient way because they are confident in who they are, where they are going, and how they are going to get there. This confidence allows them to make the best decisions for their business, even hard decisions, because they have a goal.

As an owner or manager, I get that there are many demands

on your time and energy. What if you could reduce the strain on yourself by one-half? The strain that comes from having to make daily decisions and managing curveballs that seem to endlessly come your way. How freeing would that be? This is possible by having your mission, core values, and vision in place. The advantage you will have is that you don't have to think hard about decisions that are flying in your direction, and you can spend that same energy on other things.

Think about the difference between hard and easy decisions:

- Hard decision — Should I open another location?
- Easy decision — Should I open my dealership today?
- Hard decision — Where should I invest my money?
- Easy decision — Should I have a savings account?
- Hard decision — What ice cream flavor should I get at the local ice cream store?
- Easy decision — Should I add sprinkles to my ice cream? (The answer is always yes.)

You need more easy decisions in your business. What burden would that lift for you? Maybe that becomes your mantra this year: more easy decisions. Or, just more ice cream. I think, either way, you are moving down the right path. The way you set yourself up for easy decisions is simple: know where you are going, what winning looks like, and the values you are going to exhibit to get there. And when you view every "once-in-a-lifetime opportunity" through this lens, even the most complex decisions become easier to make.

WHAT HAPPENS WHEN SOMEONE DOESN'T GET ON BOARD WITH YOUR VISION?

Every dealership we work with typically has an employee who struggles with change. Maybe it's because there have been so many changes implemented but none of them ever really stuck. I would struggle with that too. Maybe they have some insight on the situation that you don't or simply want to have some questions answered; I would want to be heard too.

One common frustration I have heard from owners and managers over the years is, "Why don't people just come in and do what you ask of them?" Here is what I have observed. We live in an age where access to information is limitless. If a person wants to understand how something works, he can figure it out in a moment. As a result, the employees who aren't immediately on board with your vision probably are not working covertly for the dealership down the road. Rather, they are simply trying to understand if you are really serious about what you're saying, and what it might look like when push comes to shove.

Maybe, just maybe, their resistance is not a definitive stance against you and what you are trying to do, but maybe it's a desire to understand your thinking.

What do you do to address this? There are three things I would encourage you to do when you have an employee who isn't on board.

1. Ask yourself, what could I do to better communicate?

Have you communicated what you are trying to do in a way that makes sense for that person? Have you explained why things are changing and how the changes will affect them?

During change, regardless of which department it affects, the number one question your people will have is "How does this affect me?" Think about any change that has happened to you in the last month. What did you want to know? My guess is the same thing your people want to know: "How does this affect me?"

Are you getting ready to implement new parts processes? Your service department wants to know, "How does this affect me?" Are you hiring a service coordinator to help with the efficiency in the service department? Everyone wants to know, "How does this affect me?" Are you going to start to look at numbers regularly by department? All your people will be a little nervous and want to know, you guessed it, "How does this affect me?"

2. Have a "walk with me" conversation, and understand their point of view.

Whenever you have an issue with an employee, you never bring up the issue in front of others. What you need to do is say, "Walk with me." Taking a walk with an employee allows you to do a few things. First, it allows the conversation to be private but still visible. When dealing with conflict, you want the conversation to be private. We always want to praise in public and correct in private, however, that doesn't mean you don't want someone else to have eyes on the situation.

When you take an employee "for a walk," you will see that you are on "neutral ground" and many times your employee's guard will go down. Their arms will unfold, and their tone will have a dramatic change, probably not like puberty level but close. This is what you want to happen. The lower the guard, the better information you can get from the employee and the closer to a solution you will get.

Bob was on-site with a dealer a few years ago when he encountered an all-too-common situation. The owner was frustrated that their service coordinator was "never doing what was asked of him." To prove the point, the owner asked the service coordinator to move a stack of pallets before lunchtime. Lunchtime came and went, and the pallets were in the same location as before; the owner was furious. Bob and the owner went to the service coordinator and asked him to take a walk with them. During this walk, Bob asked the service coordinator to help him understand what had come up that had prevented him from moving the pallets before lunch. He told them that an elderly customer came in and needed assistance. The service coordinator had thought about it and figured the owner would have wanted him to help the customer and deal with the pallets later. He was right. It lined up with their core values, but this could have never been figured out if a "walk with me" moment had not happened.

3. Set expectations going forward.

At this point, if you have communicated clearly and understood the issue by walking with the employee, it's up to you to set expectations about what appropriate behavior looks like going forward. You need to set up checkpoints, to make sure both parties are moving forward, and define and communicate clearly the consequences for not meeting expectations.

Maybe you have asked your technicians to keep their workspace clean. But, one of your technicians seems to have completely missed the memo, and every time you walk into the shop it looks like a tornado has torn through his bay. First, you need to make sure that they understand what clean means to you. The technician may have a completely different definition of clean. Then, you need to start checking in with him every day. Once you see that he understands what is expected, you can move to checking in twice a week, then once a week, and then a few times a month.

Positive change in people will happen if you take the time to follow up on the requested change and help them implement the habits to make the change stick.

YOUR SURVIVING-VERSUS-THRIVING VISION

A few years ago, my husband and I decided to get beta fish for our twin daughters. They were four years old at the time, and I had just gotten home from several weeks on the road. Did we use the possibility of buying them beta fish as bribery for them to go to bed each night for my husband? Absolutely. And it worked, but now we had to follow through.

The night I got home, we took our girls to the local pet store. They took their sweet time picking out the perfect beta fish for them, and then we went to get the fishbowls so that they could live a happy life being overfed by four-year-olds. As we were picking the fishbowls, my husband asked the lady working in the fish department if there was anything else we needed to be the proud fish owners we were destined to be. She took one quick glance at our cart, which already seemed excessively full to me, and quickly identified herself as a "fish expert." She said, with extreme judgment in her voice, "Well, it looks like you have everything you need for your fish to survive, but those fish won't thrive if you only buy what's in your cart." She then took us to the fish tanks, which were double the cost, that would allow our fish to thrive.

I wish I could tell you that this story ends with us saying that we were okay with our fish just surviving, but sixty dollars later, we had all we needed for our fish to thrive (for about three months until they went to fish heaven).

Many times, as owners and managers, your vision for your dealership can come to a place of simply surviving. Maybe your surviving vision looks like making sure you have enough money in the bank for payroll, taxes, insurance, and to pay off floor plan, all without dipping into your line of credit. I want to make it clear: if this is where you are, this is okay. It's okay that, today, you are focused on surviving. But what is not okay is staying in this place forever. The only person who has the power to make the choice for you to move to a place of a thriving vision is you. I can't decide for you; you are the one who must embrace what a thriving dealership would look like and move toward it.

Have you ever wondered why a hamster would get on the wheel and continue to subject himself to movement that doesn't result in any progress? As humans, don't we do the same thing on treadmills? But I digress. I'm sure people much smarter than I have contemplated this, but my uneducated guess lies in the fact that humans and hamsters alike believe the illusion of purpose and progress (or thriving) feels better than the hard reality that your current state is one of simply surviving.

Regardless of where you are in the surviving-versus-thriving continuum of your dealership, you are the only person who can get yourself, and your dealership, off the hamster wheel and move your dealership forward.

GETTING YOUR TEAM ON BOARD
WITH YOUR VISION FOR THE FUTURE

Remember Ron and Marsha with matching polos from the GIE+EXPO? Well, not long after that meeting with Bob, they made an intentional decision to work at bringing their team on board with the mission, core values, and vision of their dealership. Today, their employees know that the owners are committed to growing them as individuals and can make decisions that are in line with where the dealership is going. They have had virtually no turnover, and the dealership is growing and prospering.

Regardless of what you are trying to communicate with your team, stories are the most effective way to do it. People don't learn from bullet points; they learn from stories. As you communicate your mission, tell your people why you are passionate about it. Share with them the story of how you started the dealership and why. As you communicate your core values, give real-life examples about how you have seen these values at play in your dealership. And as you clarify your vision for the future of your dealership, you need to provide a scenario of how this vision is coming to reality in front of your people every single day.

The moment you walk away from utilizing stories and examples to get your people on board, you are walking away from the most powerful communication tool you have.

The choice is yours. You can choose to be in "survive mode" and just keep pushing through each day until you can't bear to do it any longer, or choose to move into "thrive mode" and be like Ron and Marsha who rediscovered their vision after many years of struggling and now are excited again about their dealership and their future.

HABIT TWO:

Be Willing to
Learn and Change

I'M THE PROBLEM: *I'm not stubborn,*
I just know my way is best.
I'M THE SOLUTION: *When you know better, you do better.*

Bob and I love stories of transformation. There is something captivating about the before-and-after that always draws us in to ask the question, "How did they do that?" Whether it's a rag-to-riches story, a weight-loss show, or a dramatic home renovation, I'm always in amazement and on the edge of my seat.

Anyone who has experienced these types of transformations will tell you it did not happen overnight. There was no "easy" button. Instead, many small changes eventually led to big results. If you want to see a lasting transformation in your dealership, you must embrace the slow, deliberate process of change.

Do you know what separates successful dealers from those who are stuck in a pattern of complacency, season after season?

They are willing to make small and deliberate changes and stick with those changes even when they aren't going as planned. It's also clear that the words "But that's how we have always done it" never come out of their mouth.

LITTLE CHANGES MAKE A BIG DIFFERENCE

Have you ever had a small rock in your shoe? I enjoy running and have spent much of my adult life running as a form of exercise and stress relief. It's a lot easier to run out your aggression than to punch someone in the face and go to jail, but again I digress. I get that, to many people, this makes me weird, but I'm okay with it.

There have been times I have put on my running shoes and immediately noticed a small rock inside. Did I put the rock there on purpose? No. But that doesn't change the fact that the rock is still there. Regardless of how the rock found its way into my shoe, all I can think about, at that moment, is that silly little rock. It doesn't matter what the weather is like or how hard my run is, this one tiny, annoying, little rock, that I did not put in my shoe, takes all of my attention.

So, what's the solution? I have to stop what I'm doing, take off my shoe, and remove the rock. Does it take time to stop, take off my shoe, and get the rock out? Yes. Is it an inconvenience? Yes.

However, within a moment, something interesting happens. The time, pain, and inconvenience caused by the rock are quickly a distant memory and I'm experiencing utter relief and able to move forward with my run.

Successful dealers understand that often the changes they need to make don't require a complete overhaul of their dealership or even a department. Most of the time the changes that need to be made are little things that have a big impact. You don't always understand how significant the impact is or how much something was weighing on you until you remove the issue. The moment you make the change, things start to become easier and the issue, like the rock in your shoe, becomes a distant memory.

A small change in your service department that will alleviate pain may include having your technicians clocking in and out of work orders. Sure, it could be an inconvenience to implement this but, after you do, the ability to understand where time is going and what you can do to change the profitability of the department will change the department as a whole.

A small change in your parts department might be the decision to burn down inventory about three months before your slow season, giving you the cash you need to survive a slower time of the year. It's not often that your employees will take parts, as payment, in place of a paycheck when business slows down, and the extra cash can make a big difference to you. Yes, you and your employees will have to learn a new skill and it will take time; however, the small amount of pain and inconvenience you experience will be paid back with increased cash flow during a historically slow time.

In whole goods, this small change could be having your salespeople track their follow-up on quotes or bids and the results they were having. As we work with dealerships, we require salespeople to make a minimum of five follow-ups on any quote or bid they have given. Why? Because studies have said that most salespeople make only one follow-up call yet on average it takes five for the average quote or bid to be accepted. Yes, it's a change from how you have done things in the past, but the effects of the change will create more consistent cash flow into your dealership throughout the year.

No one puts a rock in their shoe on purpose. My guess is that you and your team are already doing a lot of things right or you wouldn't still be in business. What will separate you from where you are and where you want to be is identifying where the rock slipped in and what you can do to get the rock out. Before you know it, the rock will be a distant memory for you and your team.

THE IMPACT OF A MOTHER ON HER SON

Tacoma is a beautiful city. It was 8:00 a.m. on a Thursday and it was our last management boot camp for the year. Sara was in the meeting room making some final adjustments to our PowerPoint; I was in the back of the room greeting dealers as they were checking in.

A young man caught my attention. He was wearing a tan baseball cap and sporting a full beard. He was probably in his early thirties. He was followed by a woman I assumed was his mother. I walked up and introduced myself to them. The woman, Rachel, told me that she was not going to attend the meeting but had paid for her son, Jason, to come. She was hoping he would bring back some ideas that he could use to convince his father to try in their dealership. I encouraged her to join us in the meeting as our guest. She thanked me for the offer, but said she had already made other plans with a friend for the morning. However, she would join us for lunch.

As Sara and I were sharing ideas on how to improve the performance and profitability in a dealership, I was intrigued with

Jason. He had an almost unquenchable thirst for what we were sharing. While he never asked any questions, he was filling his workbook with notes, underlining key points, and putting stars by the ones I am guessing he wanted to share with his father when he returned to the dealership.

It was 10:30 and time for our first break. I noticed Jason standing alone in the far corner of the room and decided it was a perfect time to learn more about him, his father, and their dealership. As we began to talk, he let down his guard and shared with me the family dynamics and the story of how his dad had started the dealership. It was dad's dream to start his own business and he did just that. His wife, Rachel, wanting to support the dream, followed along, completely unaware of the stress and difficulty that was in front of them both.

I had heard this story many times before. The two of them would end up struggling for years, with the dealership never producing the freedom and money they had dreamed of. Because the husband didn't want to fail, he dug in more and spent more hours in the business with no better results. The strain of no money and no family life led them to a point where the only thing they had in common was the young man, Jason, who was standing in front of me. Jason's parents divorced. The wife moved on, but the son wanted to stay with his father and work in the business.

Over the next few years, Rachel saw Jason heading down the same path as her ex-husband. More hours, long days, and no more money or really anything else to show for it. Rachel had, for years, been following our company and knew of the success we had with other dealers. She had tried in vain to get her ex-husband to use some of our ideas, but he refused. Desperate, when she heard we were coming to Tacoma, she paid for Jason's registration and literally put him in the car. She traveled with him to the boot camp making him promise to keep an open mind, listen to our ideas, and try to use them to help break the cycle his father and their business were in. I am a big believer that God puts us in front of people for a reason, and I knew in my heart, that I, and my team, would be taking on Jason as a project for the next twelve months if he was willing.

When it came time for lunch, Rachel arrived and joined Jason and me at our table. We filled her in on what we had covered in the morning sessions, and as we were about to finish lunch, I turned and asked a simple question: "Jason, are you willing to change?"

"In what way?" he asked.

"Are you willing to change the things you are currently doing in your dealership and implement the ideas you have learned so far today in this workshop?"

He said, "I am, but I don't know about my dad."

"It's not about your dad," I said. "The fight has gone out of his soul. He is doing things on autopilot. Are you willing to grab hold of the wheel and start directing your business down a new path? I promise, your dad will resist a little in the beginning, but with some small wins, he will quickly let you have control. So, my question again to you is, are you willing to learn and make changes?"

His mother sat in silence, looking at her son. When he said in a confident voice, "Yes," she smiled and tears formed in her eyes. I thanked Rachel for investing in her son and told her that I wanted to present an offer to her son at the end of the workshop and would like for her to be there. She promised she would, and we left to start the afternoon session.

During the afternoon break, I reached out to my team in Kansas City and asked them if they would be open to working with Jason over the next year as a part of our Dealer Success Groups. I told them it would not be a simple journey, that we would have to deal with some family struggles, but I believed we could help make this small, struggling dealership successful. True to my team, they all said yes, and at the end of the workshop, after everyone but the mother and son had left, I shared with them my proposal. I said, "If you are committed to making the changes we suggest and willing to continue to learn with the passion I have seen in you today, we would like to work with you for the next twelve months at no cost to you, your mother, or your dad. I just need you to commit to me that you will be all in." He looked at me, then his mother, and then back to me and said, "I will do whatever you tell me to do."

"That's all I can ask. Welcome to our team!"

As the year came and went, we did have some struggles with dad, as I thought we would. Probably the biggest issue was reducing the amount of lines they were handling to lines that complemented each other but did not compete against each other. Small victories turned into big victories, and both the son and his dad have turned their dealership into a strong, profitable business. By the end of the twelve months, the dad was taking time off, making great money, and in the process of building a cabin on a piece of land he had owned for years. The son is now in charge of the dealership, making the day-to-day decisions, and is still involved with us as he moves his dealership forward with plans on starting his own family.

THE PROCESS OF CHANGING STARTS WITH ASKING THE QUESTION, "WHAT'S NOT WORKING?"

Bob's right, one of the most challenging parts of implementing any change is identifying what specifically is not working in your dealership. In many situations you are so close to the problem that you have actually become friends with it. That problem (or friend) may have even earned a spot around the dinner table, and the idea that the problem is even a problem is foreign to you.

What's not working has become comfortable. It's just how things are, and there is nothing you can do about it. *Wait, what?* Let's be clear, you run and own the business. Of course there is something you can freaking do about the problem! **Address it. Change it. Do something different.** If something isn't working, it doesn't mean that you have to just put up with the problem and hope it's going to get better. I hate to be the bearer of bad news, but in business, hope is not a strategy. You read that right; there isn't enough hope to magically evaporate your problem away.

In business, action, movement, and change are strategies, but hope isn't. Yes, we can hope for the best, but inevitably, you will find yourself in the same spot you are in today because it wasn't accompanied by any action. Regardless of where you are and what the problem is, it doesn't have to be this way.

If you were to guess, what would you say is the most challenging form of change to make for a business owner? It's not a product line change, a financial change, or even when you realize that you need to change the password on all of the devices in your dealership at the same time. The most challenging change is when the change that needs to happen is a person. Especially a person who is or has become like family to you. We will visit about the impact of your people in your dealership later, but for now it's important to understand that one of the most challenging changes to make is a personnel change. On the flip side, do you know what we see as one of the most impactful changes you can make? A personnel change, especially if that person is toxic.

It doesn't matter where you are in the world, what kind of dealership you run, or how big your heart is—this is an issue for everyone and it's just plain hard. Let's be honest, dealing with toxic people is probably the part of the job that sucks the most. It's a drain on you, your other people, and your business. It can seem like the easiest solution is to not deal with it, sweep it under the rug, and hope (remember, this isn't the strategy we are using) that the problem will work itself out.

Truth bomb: people problems aren't just going to work themselves out. What will happen is that your good employees will leave and go somewhere else, leaving you with only those who drain the life and money out of you and your business. That does not sound like a good plan.

Meet a dealer who after years of implementing the "strategy of hope" made the decision to make changes. Here is how Kathy and her parents addressed a toxic personnel issue and the results they experienced.

IT STARTED WITH A PHONE CALL

"Good morning, this is Bob Clements."

"Hi, my name is Kathy," the woman on the phone call informed me, "and I need your help to fix our dealership." While this wasn't an unusual call for us to get, I could tell from her voice that she was stressed. As I asked Kathy some questions, I found that the dealership her dad and mom, Keith and Virginia, had started over fifty years ago was struggling financially to stay alive. Kathy informed me that she had come back into the business after a manufacturer canceled the dealer's contract for a major line they had carried since the start of their business. It was a devastating blow to both the dealership and her parents. While Keith and Virginia were handling the situation the best they could, everything was collapsing around them. They were at a point where they were taking their life savings and dumping it back into the business to make payroll and keep the lights on.

Kathy told me about the changes they were making in order to redefine and reset themselves from the "brand" they had maintained for the last fifty years to the new dealership they would need to become. Then I asked Kathy a question that would lead us toward finding a solution to their real problem. I asked, "So how are the employees dealing with the new changes you are trying to implement?"

She paused and then said, "Well, almost everyone is on board with what we need to do."

"Who's not on board?" I asked.

"Our parts manager, Roger," she told me. "He says he's on board when we meet with him, but then he goes back to the parts department and tells his people that the dealership is going to go broke and they should be looking for another job." When I asked why they didn't simply replace him, Kathy told me that the parts manager had been with them for over thirty years, all the customers knew him, and they had to have him to run the parts department.

Kathy's story is one I hear all too often. A long-term employee is fighting the changes the dealership needs to make, sabotaging the business, and holding the owners hostage. "Kathy," I told her, "your only option is to be clear with Roger. He needs to adjust to the changes, get his team on board, or you will find someone else who can." There was a long pause on the line and then Kathy asked if there was a way I could come and help them through this problem.

I knew at that point, Kathy needed me to convince Keith and Virginia that the parts manager would need to either change or leave the dealership. We worked out the details, and two weeks later at 8:00 a.m. on a Monday morning I arrived at the store. I spent my first day meeting with Keith, Virginia, and Kathy, learning about their history, their employees, and their new ideas for transforming their old brand to their new one. I met with their salespeople; Jim, their service manager; and Roger, who headed up the parts department. The service manager and I had a great conversation. Jim had been in that role for almost twenty years, and while he had concerns about the changes taking place, he was willing to do whatever Keith and Virginia needed to keep the dealership going. I found out from Keith that Jim had even offered to take a pay cut if it would help the dealership survive. As I met with his techs, they were a little concerned about the future, but it was apparent that Jim was a good leader and continued to meet with them, keep them updated on the changes taking place, and encourage them to stay focused on putting out good work.

Roger was a little different story. Unlike Jim, Roger used our time together to tell me everything he had done for the last thirty years to help the dealership succeed and how little he had been rewarded for all his effort. I talked to him about his pay, and how it was far above what other parts managers in similar dealerships were making. I asked him why he had stayed for so long if he felt like he was underappreciated and underpaid. Roger said, "Because I'm loyal." I smiled and asked, "Do you mean you are loyal, or just feel like you have had a pretty good deal?" With that, Roger crossed his arms and said, "Is there anything else you need from me?" There was one more thing. "I need you to make a decision as to whether or not you believe you can change your attitude, and manage and lead your team in a positive manner, like Keith and Virginia need, so that they can continue to move the dealership forward. I don't need an answer now," I said. "Take some time tonight, give it some thought, and let me know your decision tomorrow morning." With that, Roger left. I met with Keith, Virginia, and Kathy, caught them up on my conversations with both Jim and Roger, and let them know tomorrow would be an interesting day.

The next day did prove to be interesting because Roger called in sick. It worked out great because it gave me the day to really get to know the parts team and assess their talent and attitudes without concern for what Roger might think or say. I pulled Jim, along with the sales team, together with Keith, Virginia, and Kathy. We visited about how other dealerships who had gone through similar experiences had successfully adapted and how they could implement some of the same ideas in their business. I was convinced that, while everyone had some concerns, the dealership had a strong group of employees that the owners could count on to help drive the changes needed.

Wednesday was my last scheduled day at the dealership, and my last opportunity to meet again with Roger. I got there early hoping I might be able to catch him before it got busy, but that wasn't going to be the case. The moment the front door opened, customers started flowing in, phones started ringing, and the parts counter was busy. By mid-morning, things finally slowed enough that I was able to bring Roger, Keith, Virginia, and Kathy together for the conversation we all needed to have.

I started by thanking Roger for all the hard work he had put into the dealership and let him know that Keith, Virginia, and Kathy felt the same way. I then asked Roger if he felt that he could continue to support the dealership with the necessary changes and if he could be a positive force not only for his parts people but, just as importantly, to his customers. He let us know that he believed he had been positive about the changes and had not come across as negative to his team. I let him know that while I knew he believed what he said, it was not the impression I had gotten from either his people or others in the dealership.

I mentioned that Keith, Virginia, Kathy, and I had talked about the changes we needed to see in him if he was going to continue with the dealership. We explained that whether it was him or someone else, the dealership needed a strong, positive force managing the parts department if they were to have a chance of succeeding. Roger nodded his head in agreement and got up to leave. Right before he left, I said to him, "Roger, I need to make sure you understand the situation. If every day you can't walk into your department and be a positive influence on your people and work beside everyone else in the dealership to make the changes necessary, there will not be a position available for you. Is that understood? He looked at Keith, Virginia, and Kathy and then back to me saying, "So you think they would fire me?" I said,

"Roger, it's your decision if you want the job. Everything about this job is in your control. Whether you choose to stay or leave, it's all up to you."

Roger turned and walked out of the meeting room and headed to his office. After he left, Keith spoke up and said, "What if he chooses to leave?"

"He may," I said, "and I would bet money that he wasn't sick yesterday but putting feelers out for other jobs. I had an opportunity to spend time with your parts people yesterday and was very impressed with David. He is sharp, the other parts people look up to him, and he is passionate about you three and the dealership. If Roger decides to walk, I would move David into his role and I don't think you will miss a beat."

I finished the afternoon and headed to the airport. I was not exactly sure how things would play out, but I knew, either way, the dealership was headed in a positive direction. I continued to touch base with them, and over the next couple of weeks, Roger seemed to still be struggling. About four weeks after my visit, I received a call from Kathy. She told me Roger had turned in his two-week notice and that he was going to work as a parts person for another dealership. I suggested that Kathy calculate Roger's remaining vacation time and, at the end of the day, have his check ready for the vacation time he was due and the hours he had worked to that point. Thank him for his work and ask for his keys and company credit card. I then asked her to find a time we could schedule a webcast so that she, her parents, and I could discuss next steps.

At 11:00 that morning the four of us met. I recommended that they move David, the young man I had met a month ago, into

Roger's role. They agreed and then I asked Kathy to bring David into our meeting. As Kathy was getting David, I asked Keith and Virginia how they were feeling. Keith was unsure that David could replace Roger, and Virginia told me she had known the day would come that Roger would leave and was just glad it was over. As Kathy and David came in, Kathy shared with David what Roger had told them this morning. David didn't look surprised. I said, "David, I am guessing you were aware that Roger was looking?"

"Yes," he said. "He told us all a couple of weeks ago that he was interviewing at another dealership and if they had other openings, he would try to get us hired."

"David, we appreciate your honesty and openness," I said, "and we would like for you to consider taking on Roger's role as parts manager. You don't have to tell us this moment. I would like you to give it some serious thought tonight, talk to your wife, and give us your answer tomorrow." The next day, I got a call from Kathy saying David was excited to take on the role. He had talked to the other parts people and they were excited to be working with him.

Over three years have passed since that first call with Kathy. The dealership has turned the corner and rebranded itself. Jim and the service department are doing great work with fast turnarounds. The salespeople have embraced the new line their dealership took on and are seeing strong growth. David and his team have transformed the parts department. The counter is spotless, and the parts displays are full of products that sell. He is on top of his parts returns. He has reduced the parts inventory on hand by almost $80,000, has improved parts margins by 3 percent, and is a positive force every day for the dealership, their customers, and his team.

Within days of making the change, getting rid of the conflict, stress, and burden created by just one person, everyone's attitudes and optimism returned. Kathy and her parents couldn't believe the almost immediate impact this change had made not only on their own level of excitement but also on their entire team.

Is changing people difficult? Sure it is. But after all these years I will tell you that, more often than not, getting rid of negative people and those who are holding you hostage, regardless of how long they have been with your dealership, will bring a positive change to your store.

Are you ready to look at things from a new perspective and make some changes? If yes, then repeat after me. *If it doesn't make me money, I will stop doing it or find a way for it to make me money.*

Think about each department in your dealership. Now, ask yourself, is every department actually generating profit? Everything you or your people touch should make money. You didn't start your dealership as a non-profit for your community, but so many of you are running them that way.

Let's walk through three departments (service, parts, and sales) with Sara and discuss where we commonly see dealers lose money and how those who are open to learning and changing can fix it.

SERVICE

The service department is an area that is near and dear to Bob's and my hearts. Why? Because this is typically what many dealers refer to as the "dark hole of hell that even Satan himself doesn't want to enter." What we know for sure is that if you can get the processes right in service, it can generate you more revenue than any other department in your dealership. When we begin working with a dealer, it is quite common to find that the service department is actually costing them money to keep it open. And, the fact of the matter is, this isn't how you should run a profitable dealership. (Thank you, Captain Obvious!)

There are several ways you can increase efficiency and profitability in the service department. I have outlined four below that will get you started.

Technicians Clocking In and Out of Work Orders

Everything in your service department is based on time. You will not be able to see progress in your service department if you don't know where the time you are buying is going. In your service department, your inventory is time. You buy eight hours of inventory each day per technician you employ, but most dealers have no idea where the inventory goes. That is why we track every tenth of an hour, or every six minutes, in a service department.

That's right, we track and account for every six minutes. We do this because even a little bit of time makes a big difference. Let's say your labor rate is $100 an hour for the sake of easy math. Each tenth of an hour is worth $10—that's simple enough. For this example, imagine that you have one technician and he loses one billable hour throughout each day. You know, a tenth of an hour here and there. That would mean that over the course of a month, your department would be losing $2,000 a month, or $24,000 a year. That is money out of your pocket simply because they lost track of an hour per day. And that's just one technician! There should be no reason why your technicians are not clocking in and out; for us, this is a deal breaker and the reason to move out a technician or service manager who refuses to do it.

At one point, one of our BCI advisors was on-site at a dealership in Texas. He was working with the service department to establish the process of clocking in and out of work orders, when a technician came up to him and said, "My wife doesn't keep track of where I am and what I'm doing. What makes you think you can keep track of my time?" It's safe to assume this man was probably not a long-term employee of the dealership, but it didn't change the fact that we still required him to track his time like everyone else.

So, how do you do this? If you have dealer management software in place, use the time clock or service module you are probably already paying for. This is the easiest way to track the time in your service department and pull the numbers you need to understand the health of your dealership. We will talk about the numbers you need to track later, but if you have the functionality use it!

If you don't have software in place that allows your technicians to clock in and out of work orders, you can start tracking time with a pad of paper and a clock. You will simply require your technicians to write down the work order or repair order number, and what they are doing with their time as they are doing it.

Technicians are notoriously terrible at keeping track of time, so, at first, this change is going to be a shock. But the more aware you and your technicians become of time, the more profitable the service department will be.

Work with your techs to create this new habit. Establish it as the expectation and reinforce it daily. This change is a game-changer, but the change begins with you and you requiring it to happen.

Clean Up the Crap in Your Service Department and Organize Your Lot

We have been in hundreds and hundreds of service departments around the country, and we know the amount of crap you keep there. If you hope to have a highly efficient and profitable service department, you have to get rid of all the junk. Honestly, they could start a show called *Hoarders: The Dealership Edition* and have a hit series on their hands.

I want you to pause the work in your service department for one day and have an all-hands-on-deck moment where you clean up the service area as a team. While this may cost you a small amount of money in lost revenue in the short run, you will regain it quickly through increased efficiency and an organized shop.

As you are a business owner, I know this sounds painful for several reasons.

First, as you look at the stuff in your shop you may just see dollar signs and it kills you to think about throwing things away. I get it, you don't want to get rid of it. We have seen it all. We have seen engines with cracked blocks, old carburetors, a million odd nuts and bolts, fiberglass golf car bodies that were cracked and replaced, old rotting tires; literally if it had once been attached to a unit in the shop, we have seen dealerships save these items because maybe, just maybe, they will need it at some point. That stuff hasn't been touched in years and it is costing you money. Think about it this way: your technicians will make you more money by having a clean, unobstructed space to work, much more than you could possibly gain from the clutter and junk you are hanging on to, I promise.

Second, the idea of spending the day cleaning doesn't necessarily sound like fun. Just because it's not fun doesn't mean it shouldn't be done. Let me walk you through, step by step, how you are going to clean out the buried treasure in your service department.

1. First, **take everything out of your service department.** There should be nothing on the floor. Yes, I mean everything is moved outside. There should be no shop towels or old filters. Not a barrel or bag of floor dry. No wood blocks, jack stands, or even floor jacks. Everything is out. While it might not be clean at this point, it will be empty.

2. Now, with everything out, **decide what does *not* belong in the shop**. Our rule of thumb is if you haven't touched it for six months, you should sell it or *throw it away*. Anything that you don't need and can't be sold for at least twenty dollars, throw it away. This includes extra old used parts that have been lying around forever. They need to be gone. If you do have a compelling reason to not toss an item (maybe it's been there so long you have named it and count it as one of your friends), you must come up with an actual plan to sell it. Once you identify what you haven't touched in six months, look at everything else and ask, "Is this necessary to run the service department?" If the answer is no, sell it if it's metal and throw it away if it's not. Oh, and if you don't have a dumpster, you're going to need to rent one. Harsh, I know, but you needed someone to tell it like it is.

3. Once everything is out of the service department, it's time to **power-wash floors.** When you have everything cleared out and your floors are power-washed, something amazing will happen. You will magically have more space. Every dealership who does this feels like they have an abundance of space after this step, and you will too. You want to make the most of the newfound space, and painting lines for bays is an inexpensive way to give your technicians ownership of their space.

    If it's in the budget, I would also encourage you to provide each technician with dealership-issued toolboxes. This not only helps with the overall look and uniformity of the service department, but it also maximizes the space you have available. It also makes it harder for a technician to get mad, pack up their tools, and simply leave.

4. The final part is to bring everything that is necessary back into your service department. **Everything must have a home**—jack stands, floor jacks, floor dry, gas cans, shop towels, specialty tools—everything.

    Keep in mind that nothing is going to come back into the shop that doesn't have an assigned spot. This is nonnegotiable. If you bring something back in and just throw it anywhere, you are only adding to the problem you had in the first place.

Now Focus Your Attention on Your Lot

There is nothing more embarrassing than to have a customer call your service department to check on their unit and you don't actually know where it is. Let's face it, when you are in season and the units needing service and repair are flooding into your dealership, things can get a little disorganized. The common phrase we hear during season when units are being dropped off is, "Just find an empty space and put it there." It's not long before units that are in for service are getting mixed up with units that need to be repaired and the chaos begins. One of the key pieces of our service process utilizes a color-coded system. We use this approach in every service department we work with to indicate where each unit is at in the process. We use flagging ribbon and cattle tags for quick reference. These items withstand all types of weather. They are durable and hard to mess up. We buy a lot of these for the dealerships we work with. The veterinarian supply company that we purchase from are under the impression that we are one of the largest cattle producers in the country.

We have created a specific system for tagging and flagging units, and we utilize this process during triaging and throughout the service or repair of each unit. For a detailed list of which color of ribbon we assign to the different stages of the process and why, along with companies you can order tags and ribbon from, go to the free resources quick link on our website (bobclements.com), or check out the appendix in the back of the book.

The most important thing that organizing your shop and lot will do is save you time, and, as we talked about earlier, time is money in the service department. An additional benefit is that you will reduce frustration for yourself, your service team, and your customers when you can find units easily and have a process in place you can rely on.

File Your Warranty Claims

We were recently working with a dealership that was struggling with cash flow. We asked the owner when the last time his service manager had filed warranties with this manufacturer was, and it had been a few months. When we looked at the open warranty work orders, we found he was sitting on over $30,000 of unfiled warranty claims, which was the cash flow he desperately needed.

You have probably been in a similar situation and have had a stack of unfiled warranty claims sitting on your desk. It's not because you had a disdain for filing warranties (or on the other hand, maybe you do). Maybe you've been extremely busy and it was just overlooked. You pull the "I'll get to it later" card, and before you know it you are thousands of dollars behind in warranties.

Let's face it—most manufacturers do a good job paying you for the warranty work you do, if you are filing on time like you are supposed to. Take an objective look at where you are with warranties. Are you up to date with your claims? If not, how much cash flow are you sitting on as we speak? Come up with a plan to fix this and pick up that all-important cash flow you need.

PARTS

Let's switch gears and focus on what changes might be required in the parts department to begin to increase profitability. We consider the service department to be the backbone of the dealership and the parts department the lifeblood that runs through the dealership. There is very little that happens in the dealership, from the first interaction with customers to supporting all areas of the dealership, that doesn't involve the parts department. We often joke that *Service is a science* and *Parts is an art*. So, channel your inner Picasso, and together let's look at your parts department from a fresh perspective.

There are several changes you can make in the parts department that will have a major impact. For today, I am going to focus on three that are pretty easy to implement: the proper placement of your fastest-moving parts, management of your parts pricing, and implementing up-selling and cross-selling. Let's look at these one at a time.

Check the Placement of Your Fastest-Moving Parts

One simple change is to evaluate and adjust the placement of your fastest-moving parts. Using your dealer management software, you have the ability to pull a report that identifies your fastest-moving parts. Using this information, you will want to find a way to physically move these parts as close as possible to the point of sale, so that when a customer comes in for one of fifty or a hundred parts they are just a step away.

Many times, a parts department will take a high-density parts cabinet and put it right under or right behind the parts counter. While these can be an investment in the beginning, you will find that when properly stocked, they can, in many cases, replace a part-time person. We also find that these parts cabinets don't require health insurance, need vacation time, and never, ever show up late for work.

Doing this will increase the efficiency of your parts people and decrease transaction time. We will talk about transaction time a little bit more when we look at the numbers in Habit Four, but transaction time is a number you should track in your parts department that simply tells you the total amount of time it takes for a customer to enter your store and walk away with the parts they need. You can easily track this number with the stopwatch on your phone and a piece of paper and pen. (Again, more on this coming up!)

The transaction time in your parts department will vary based upon what products you carry; however, a general rule of thumb is that you want the transaction time less than twelve minutes. Sure, twelve minutes doesn't seem like a long time if you are at the counter, but if you are the fifth person in line, twelve minutes a person will seem like forever. Make a commitment to organize your parts department so that the fastest-moving parts can be reached quickly, helping to increase efficiency and reduce the number of angry parts customers (that is, unless you love angry parts customers).

Next, Price Your Parts Correctly

When thinking about margins, the first thing you need to keep in mind is that the margins on your parts should not be at MSRP. You read that right. MSRP is simply what the manufacturer suggests the retail price on the part should be, and sometimes the suggestion doesn't fit with your pricing strategy.

While your target margin for your parts varies based upon the lines and product mix you carry, the margins on most of your parts should be above MSRP. When you look at MSRP, you have to keep in mind that it is set based on turning your parts four times a year. If you aren't turning a part that consistently, you need to make sure that your margins reflect that because it is taking up valuable space on your shelves.

A dealer recently told me that she didn't know that their pricing was supposed to be above MSRP because no one had ever told her. Listen, this is me telling you your parts margins on items that are turning less than four times per year should, in most cases, be above MSRP!

There are a couple of simple ways to move your margins up on parts. One way is called matrixing or tier pricing, and you do it by adding percentages over MSRP based upon price points. As an example, if a part sells for anything less than one dollar you might mark it up 200 percent. If it sells for $1.01 to $2.50 you might consider marking it up 150 percent over MSRP. If the part sells for $2.51 to $5.00, maybe it's 140 percent, and so on. As the price goes up, the markup goes down so that around the $50.00 range you are back at MSRP.

A second approach is called velocity pricing. You use this pricing strategy after you have put into place your matrix or tiered pricing. With velocity pricing, you select a few items that are price sensitive and go slightly below MSRP and then showcase those parts on your parts counter or endcaps.

To offset the lost profit by going below MSRP, you handpick parts that people are generally unaware of or unconcerned with the price of the item and move them up more aggressively in your matrix pricing. Your goal is to balance the profit lost by going below MSRP on a few items with the extra profit gained on select prices by going above your matrix pricing strategy.

Finally, Train Your People on How to Upsell and Cross-Sell at the Parts Counter

One change that has the potential to fundamentally alter your parts department in a positive way is to think differently about the role of the people who work there. You need to help your parts staff begin thinking of themselves as counter parts *salespeople*. That's right, they are salespeople. I get the apprehension that comes with the word *salesperson*, but if your parts people start for even a minute to think about themselves in that context instead of order takers, something amazing happens. First, your sales will increase, and second, your customers will have a better experience. Both outcomes should be two of the top goals for every parts departments.

So, how do you do this? First, you have to begin training them to think of themselves as salespeople, and one of the easiest ways to do that is through teaching the techniques of upselling and cross-selling at the parts counter.

Have you ever been through a drive-thru of a fast-food restaurant (oh please, you feed your kids chicken nuggets too!) and been asked the question, "Do you want fries with that?" Unless you have adhered to a strict kale and celery diet your entire life, I'm sure you have heard that question before. If that is the case, we are all collectively sad for you. When you are asked the question, "Would you like fries with that?" the person at the drive-thru window is cross-selling you. They are saying, people who bought what you are buying (cheeseburger) typically also bought this (fries). They are creating a better experience for you, as they are making sure that you are getting everything you might want or need.

Maybe you have worked on a Saturday plumbing job that required a trip to the hardware store. How many times did that one trip to the hardware store turn into two or three trips, because you forgot to pick up one thing that seemed like common sense? You would have been thrilled if a salesperson at the store had told you that when people bought a new faucet, they normally replaced the water cut-off valves at the same time. Many customers will also replace the old lines that hooked up to the old faucet with new ones as well. For someone else, their experience may have been a paint and a paintbrush, or dirt and a shovel, or even a new grill and charcoal. Regardless, when your people cross-sell at the parts counter, it makes the customer's experience better. (Fact: Customers typically don't get happier the more times they have to return to get one job done.)

So, you start helping your parts counter salespeople start thinking about cross-selling. For example, if someone comes in for oil filters, they might ask if they need oil as well. It's not complex, but approximately 30 percent of the time, the customer will go ahead and say yes to the fries, I mean oil.

Upselling is another technique that allows the customer an opportunity to buy a bigger or better version of the product they came in to purchase. This is the equivalent of going through the drive-thru and the person at the window asks if you would like to make your meal a larger size. For a little bit more money, you can get a substantially better product or a better value.

It's not uncommon for us to see parts counter salespeople upselling batteries. A customer may come in and say, "Give me the cheapest battery you have." If you were upselling, you would help them understand the advantages of spending a little more money to buy a better battery.

Upselling is an education process for the customers, allowing them to understand how a little more money will provide more value and a better experience.

There are a number of other ways that you can continue to improve the efficiency and overall profitability of the parts department, but the three we have outlined are a great place to start. By beginning with small changes you and your parts staff will begin to see movement and profitability in your parts department.

SALES

Just like service and parts, your sales department plays an important role in generating the cash flow that will give your dealership long-term and profitable growth. One of the most overlooked areas in the sales department is the actual tracking of customer contacts, new leads, and quotes by the dealership's salespeople. To do this effectively your sales team must utilize the portion of your dealership's software referred to as the CRM or Customer Relationship Management system.

Utilize Your CRM to Improve Sales Profits

The CRM is simply a database of all your customers, both past and current. Anyone who has done business with you. The information the CRM provides is extremely valuable for your salespeople so they can track and manage all of the leads being produced by your marketing efforts, and keeps them on schedule as they follow up and work to bring the quotes to a close. From a marketing perspective, your CRM gives you valuable information on both your customers' likes and needs as well as provides insight as to what effect your marketing efforts are having on generating new customers for the dealership. As a management tool, the CRM allows you to look at the number of contacts it takes for each salesperson to move a person from a quote to a close and gives you important insight on how each salesperson is doing individually so that you can determine future training needs. If your software doesn't currently have a CRM as a part of it, I encourage you to ask your software provider to build it as a part of a future update. If it is going to be a while before that happens, consider looking online for a third-party program that you can use in the short term. If you want to maximize your sales and marketing efforts, a CRM is a must-have for your dealership and a change worth pursuing.

Partner with Service and Parts to Improve Margins

In today's world of sales, almost everyone wants to negotiate price. And, while you can get away from it at some level, the reality is you don't want to lose a sale, not only because it adds dollars to the bottom line in the short term, but it adds future parts and service business to the dealership in the long-term, which improves the lifetime value of a customer. The key when negotiating is to use something other than cash, something that has some margins built into it. The best way to negotiate is to leverage your parts and service departments. Think about creating parts and service packages as negotiation tools rather than cash. While negotiating using cash is the easy way to make a sale, but you are also giving up net profit dollars that have no margins. One hundred dollars in cash costs you exactly one hundred dollars. Yet that same one hundred dollars in parts might only cost you sixty dollars because of your margins, or in service that one hundred dollars might only cost you forty dollars. We encourage the dealerships we work with to have the service and parts department get together and build out service packages for all the different units you sell. Almost every piece of equipment or unit you sell will have a manufacturer's recommended first service based upon either hours or miles. Depending upon the unit, it might run from one hundred dollars up to five hundred dollars. Regardless, by having those first service packages built out in advance with pricing, you are giving your salesperson a negotiating tool they can use instead of cash, which is a big win for your dealership.

Will this take time and effort? There is no question. Your salespeople will need to think differently and work on using a different set of negotiation skills when they are asked, "Can I get it for less?" Yes, you will need to give the department managers time to develop service packages. Yes, it will involve being open to a new and better method, but these steps will move you toward becoming a dealer whose people are willing to adapt to change in order to benefit the dealership as a whole.

Training, Training, Training

It's an interesting fact that most salespeople in dealerships have never been through an actual sales class or even read a book on how to sell. While your manufacturers have product training available, few programs, if any, actually teach your salespeople how to qualify a prospect, do walk-arounds, handle objections, or even close a sale. So, is it any wonder that most salespeople only close about 30 percent of all the qualified leads they work with?

One of the easiest ways to improve your profits in sales is to have better trained salespeople. There are a wide variety of sales courses available online for free and thousands of sales books that have been written on everything from the sales process, reading customers, negotiating, handling objections, and closing the sale. As we work with dealerships, we hold sales training classes for their salespeople every month to teach them not about their products but about the basics of selling. We encourage dealers to do weekly training with their people. As an owner or manager, pull your people together for thirty minutes once a week and have them each do a walk-around on something they sell. Have them go over the closes they use to move customers forward. Give the price objections and have them demonstrate to you how they overcome those objections. Quiz them on what negotiation packages they have at their disposal and let them show you how they would integrate those packages into a sale.

Selling is a profession that requires constant work to sharpen and hone the skills needed to generate revenue and increase margins. By making training a regular part of your weekly meeting with your salespeople, you will begin seeing improved closing ratios and better margins that will add value dollars to your bottom line.

Product training also places demands on your time. A simple way to maximize and simplify your product training demands is to reduce the number of competing lines you handle. Each new line you carry eats up your focus and your floorplan. It was a battle that Jason had to work through with his dad. His dad believed that anytime a line came open from another dealer, he should grab it so no one else could get it. It wasn't long before he had a little bit of everything but not a lot of anything. With each new line, he had to learn new manufacturer programs, learn floorplan programs, and send his techs to additional training. I am glad to say that during that first year with us, Jason's dad let go of the idea of hanging on to too many lines. Now, because of this change, they are making more money and reducing the amount of product training and expenses for the dealership.

Once you identify what isn't working, you are then put to the test. Do you have the tenacity to try something new?

In my opinion, the hardest part of implementing any change isn't implementing the change right out of the gate. The hardest part of implementing a change is keeping up with it when it feels like you just can't get it right. It is extremely difficult to stay with it, when all you want to do is go back to the old way of doing things because at least you know what to expect with the "old way."

The first few times, the change is new, exciting, and fun, but after that, the fun wears off and then you decide if it's something you are actually committed to. At that point you have the power to separate yourself from every other dealer who has tried and decided that, "This is the way things have always been, and it's not so bad." The "it's not so bad" mentality reeks of complacency and seems like an exhausting way to live your life and run a business.

What would you say to yourself if you were in my shoes? Probably the same thing I'm going to say to you now. That's not the way to run your business or your life. No. You can't be okay with "just okay" if you want to be successful. You have to make the decision, even when it's really, really hard, that you are going to get back up and try again until you get it right.

- When your technicians get upside down in the shop, try again.
- When you don't hit your sales goals, try again.

- When you have to dip into your credit line because business is slow, try again.
- When you are at the end of your rope, and you're not sure you can deal with the business, your people, or your customers another day, I want you to muster the strength deep in your soul and try again.

What you are doing is not easy. I don't want to gloss over it and make you think that I have any preconceived notion that if you read this book and implement these principles everything will be easy. That's not true. You will still have issues, but there will be fewer of them. It all comes down to the fact that every single time it gets hard, we have to ask ourselves the question, "What can I do differently so that next time this will be just a little less painful?" Let's pursue that. (You are the problem and the solution.)

HABIT THREE:

Understand and Apply Resources

I'M THE PROBLEM: *It's just easier if I do it myself.*
I'M THE SOLUTION: *Relationships are my best resource.*

Reach For The Stars!" That was the message on the banners hanging from the hotel balcony, on the handouts, and the floor signs that the manufacturer had put up for their National Dealer Meeting. Sara and I were invited to keynote the meeting and participate in a panel discussion later in the day.

It was 2:00 and time for the panel discussion. We were joined on the panel by five of the top-performing dealers. We would be answering questions from the dealers who were waiting to find out what the silver bullet was they had been missing and that would propel their dealership to the stars! The moderator asked us prepared questions and then opened up the meeting to take questions from the floor. This is always the fun time; you never know what will be asked. Dealers walked up to a microphone and asked us questions about hiring, compensation, adding locations, selling their business, and marketing. We had time for one final question. A couple, Justin and Abby, approached the mic and shared that they were in the process of taking over a family business. Justin asked, "Bob, if you could only give us one piece of advice as we take over the business, what would it be?"

Wow. What a great question. Boiling a response down to just one piece of advice made it a little difficult. A dealer I have known for many years came to mind. His name is Scott and he had been on quite a journey over the years.

Scott is a dealer I work with from the South. He has had to overcome many challenges including the death of his partner and having to work through buying back the dealership from his partner's wife. He has battled multiple seasons of dry weather, the financial crisis, and one of his best salespeople leaving and going to work for a competitor. If it could have happened, it has happened to this dealer.

He dealt with everything by smartly leveraging all the resources around him; he utilized the resources of the manufacturers he sold for, his banker, his accountant, the SBA, my team and me, and he even leveraged the tool truck guys who stopped by to see the techs each week. One of them led him to find the service manager he has today.

Scott is a master at reaching out to the right people for help and advice and taking advantage of the resources he has available. He doesn't let his pride or ego get in the way of what he is trying to accomplish. He is not afraid to admit he doesn't always have the answer, and he is smart enough to know that someone he knows or works with will. The other thing about Scott is, he doesn't fight advice; instead he takes it and runs with it, making adjustments and tweaks so that it will work for him and his team.

Scott and his team embrace the training resources in service, parts, and sales he has available for him. They don't just skim through training; they discuss it and put action plans in place to make it work for their store.

If there is co-op money available for marketing and promotions, he uses it all and will ask for more. Interestingly enough, because he is working hard to utilize what the manufacturers provide, they will normally find a way to give him more. Scott also understands that his people's talents are a resource he can use to help the dealership succeed. When he needs something to be done, whether it's signage inside the dealership, work on one of his service trucks, or finding a caterer for a dealership events, he goes to his people, lets them know his needs, and encourages them to use their connections and resources to help the dealership out. His people love it! They are excited to help in any way they can.

Scott has more than an average working relationship with his banker and accountant. When he was struggling during the downturn in the economy, he set up a lunch meeting with both of them and explained his challenges and the actions he was taking in the dealership to reduce expenses and improve profits. He asked the accountant to share with the banker the changes he was making and the impact it was having on the bottom line. His banker appreciated that Scott was making adjustments before they were needed and that they were on the same page. The three of them still meet once a quarter for lunch just so he can keep his bank in tune with potential needs in the future. Years earlier, when Scott and his partner started the business, they joined their dealer association. After his partner's death, Scott was able to work with the association's legal counsel to deal with the changes that needed to take place as well as utilizing their financial counsel. They were able to help him put a value on the business that would allow him to be fair to his partner's wife while keeping the dealership financially viable. Scott has worked with my team for years now and utilizes us to help find and hire employees, to improve his processes, and sometimes for just a friendly ear to share both good news as well as other new challenges he is facing.

When I hear dealers talk about their struggles and how they don't know if they will be able to overcome them, Scott always pops in my mind. I looked down at Justin and Abby, who were about to begin their dealership journey, and said, "Every dealership has dozens of resources available to them. During the times when a dealer struggles with the unknown, most let their ego and pride get in the way of using them. Justin and Abby, don't let that be you."

WHAT'S THE BIG DEAL
ABOUT RESOURCES ANYWAY?

Bob's right. When you think about the resources available to you and your dealership, what comes to mind? Resources you pay for? Outside partners, trainers, or consultants? The manufacturers or the local associations? If any of those come to mind, you would be right. Indeed, they are some of the resources you need to be utilizing.

The most successful dealers all have this in common; they take advantage of every resource at their disposal. That's right.

Every single one of them. They actively seek counsel and direction (because they know they don't know it all). They work with other dealers and their manufacturers. They are aware that some of the best ideas will come from outside their industry. They look to see what's working, and then instead of fighting it or coming up with every reason it won't work, they find a way to make it work for them. Successful dealers understand that listening to different perspectives and allowing others to speak into their business is what moves them forward.

Do you want to know the ultimate secret to utilizing resources? It's not a top-secret phone number you call in the midst of losing your ever-loving mind. It's not a website with all the information you could ever need, while that would be nice. It comes down to relationships. Relationships take time and energy to be formed and developed. Think about it this way: If a person off the street came into your dealership and asked you to help jump-start their car, would you? Probably you would (unless your heart is made of coal) because you are a kind human being. Most people are willing to help a stranger as long as it's not overly inconvenient for them. On the flip side, if a member of your family called and said they were thirty minutes away and needed their car jump-started, what would you do? Probably hop in the car, regardless of what you were doing, and go help. Would you do the same thing for a stranger? Probably not. The difference is that you have spent time developing a relationship, and trust, with your family, and the stranger is just another person to you. When you have a bond with someone, they are likely to go the extra mile for you and they know you would do the same for them. Dealers who use the resources available to them understand that it's not about the physical resources they are using. Dealers like Scott know that what makes resources powerful are the people behind the resources. Because of this, they are willing to put in the work required to develop those relationships.

As a dealer, you will have three main categories of resources available: the people you employ, your manufacturers, and other people in and around your industry.

Let's start with the resources inside your dealership.

YOUR PEOPLE

So, what is your team capable of? If you think about it, the most powerful resource you have to build or grow your business are the people you pay to work with you. (If you would just get out of their way and let them work. Let me explain.)

Your people are your most powerful resource. (Wait, my people?)

When I talk to owners and managers about the power of their team, regardless of its size, many times their eyes glaze over and they say, "Sara, that's nice, but you don't know my people." You're right. I don't, but our team knows thousands of other people just like yours. And when the owners or managers get out of their way and let them do their job, they can become unstoppable. Ouch, did that hurt?

I'll say it again, for the people in the back. The most powerful resources you have in your dealership are the people you pay to be at your dealership every single day. That's right, your employees. No one has a more in-depth look or better insight into your dealership than the people who show up every single day. The struggle is that often, as an owner, you don't want to let go of control. There, I said it. Most dealership owners and managers we work with (over five thousand of you) are control freaks. You have hired highly capable people to take things off your plate, but you never actually let them help you in the way you need.

Our focus here is on one thing—how to fully utilize your people. Don't dismiss this idea too quickly. If you want to change the direction of your business, take an objective look at who on your team is willing and able to move your dealership forward.

Have you ever driven on an icy road before? Specifically, a road covered in black ice where everyone travels half the speed limit just to get to the grocery store and stock up on toilet paper that they don't actually need? Our team is based out of Kansas City, Missouri, right in the middle of the United States. In what seems like a day, we can experience ninety-degree heat, followed by a tornado, and then, before we know it, we are in the midst of a snowstorm.

Regardless of the weather event, what typically shuts down our city is ice. When you drive on ice, you utilize a different driving technique than what is needed for any other time on the road. When you are learning to drive in Missouri, it's not uncommon for a driving instructor to take you to a big open parking lot the morning after an ice storm occurs and spend a significant amount of time teaching you to drive on the dangerous road.

When you drive on ice, your natural tendency is to tense up and grip the wheel with strength that would rival the Hulk. In reality, to safely drive on ice you need to relax, slow down, and have a comfortable grip on the wheel. (I'm sure when you picked up this book, you didn't know you were going to get lessons on how to drive on ice, but you're welcome.)

As an owner or manager, when things start moving into panic mode and getting out of control, you typically match the level of panic and hold the pieces of the business closer to you. Your grip gets tighter, much like inexperienced drivers on ice. You don't let others help with the problem because you are convinced that you are the only one capable of dealing with it.

Let's Delegate

First, you need to come to grips with the fact that you can't do it all and that's okay. That's why you have hired people to help you. Maybe they won't know exactly how to help you in the beginning, so you may need to teach and guide them, like the instructor teaching an inexperienced driver how to handle black ice on a road.

You didn't hire the people you have brought on to your team because you enjoy having increased overhead. You hired people to perform specific tasks or jobs that needed to be moved from your plate to someone else's so you could focus on running the business. If you hadn't made the decision to give up, or delegate, some control over certain functions of the dealership, you could have never gotten to where you are today.

Let's talk about the elephant in the room. For some the mention of delegation may have just sent you into a panic that caused you to revert to the fetal position, because you, like most of your employees, have had a terrible experience with delegation in the past. Perhaps your daily motto in business and in life has become "It's just easier if I do it myself." Bless your heart, if you continue to only do things yourself, the only thing that will be easy for you to achieve is burnout.

Think about it. When you hired your first employee, why did you do it? It was probably because you no longer could handle the entire load of what was required. You were tired, overwhelmed, and at capacity. (How different is that from where you are today?) However, the more people you add to your team, the further you get away from understanding that the sole reason you add people is to delegate tasks so you can do other things in the dealership that only you can do.

So, what should you be doing during the day? Well, it depends. We talked at the beginning of the first chapter about the three things all owners need to do. (As a quick reminder: 1) Cast a vision for the future. 2) Put a strategy in place for your vision. 3) Develop people to implement the strategy.) Depending on the size of your dealership, this may be all you do.

Maybe you are currently the best parts person, best salesperson, best service coordinator, and best technician you have. In that case, I need you to narrow the list down to only what you can do. On a separate piece of paper, or in the margin of the book (go ahead and write in the book, I won't tell), I want you to write down three things that only you can do in the dealership. Just three things that no one else on your team can replicate.

Your list will be unique to you. As things are today, maybe you are the only one who can make hiring or firing decisions, or maybe you are the only one who can submit warranties or work with your manufacturers or a million other things. Regardless, I want you to identify just three things only you can do. Your goal is to slowly move tasks from your plate to the other people on your team. Understand, this isn't something that is going to happen all at once, but it will happen over time.

So, pick one thing you are going to move off your plate. This is a task that you are currently doing, that is not on your top three list, and that you can equip someone else to do. Go ahead and write that task, job, or responsibility down. I know this is incredibly painful for someone who likes control, but it will be worth it. This task can be big or small, I just need you to pick one thing.

Picking the Right Person for the Job

Now that you've selected a task, you need to figure out who you are going to delegate the task to. Easier said than done, right?

There are three questions you need to ask that will help you know who to delegate a task to:

1. Who has the *ability* to do the task?
2. Do they have the *capacity* to do the task?
3. Do I trust them?

Each of these has to do with you. Remember, the focus of this chapter is you, not your employees.

1. WHO HAS THE ABILITY TO DO THE TASK?

This question forces you to look at the skills required for the task. You might find that no one else besides you currently has the skills needed, but the best part of that is skills can be taught. Even if your employee doesn't have the ability (or skills) to do the task right now, they can learn. Boom. Regardless of what skill is required, I'm confident there is training available to help your employees. Maybe, in the beginning, you are the training resource, the driving instructor. Keep in mind that any time that you invest in this employee will pay off in big ways, because something will come off of your plate and you will be on your way to reclaiming your sanity, life, and dealership, which is our goal.

2. DO THEY HAVE THE CAPACITY TO DO THE TASK?

As you are thinking about delegating a task to an employee, it's important to look objectively at how full their plate already is. Ask yourself, "Does this person have time to take on another task or project and still be able to maintain their other job functions?" If the answer is yes, great, let's get moving! If the answer is no, then we need to find someone else who can take something off their plate to free up some of their time. Your people can become delegation ninjas if we first show them how.

Just like you, most people's instinct is not to delegate. It's a skill you need to help your people develop, and the best way for them to learn is seeing you model it.

3. DO YOU TRUST THEM?

If you don't trust your employees, you will never actually delegate anything. Again, this is not an employee issue. This is a you issue. Trust is something you build with another person over time. If you don't trust your people, is it because you haven't worked at building trust to start with, or did something happen to cause you to lose the trust that was once there? If the trust with an employee is beyond repair, then you need to be honest with yourself as a manager and determine if this person can remain on the team.

How do you build trust? In its simplest form, it comes down to three questions.

Do you and your employee understand where you are each coming from? When developing trust, your people want to know that you understand where they are coming from and you need to understand their perspective. It doesn't mean you or they have to agree, but simply understand.

Can you count on each other's thought processes? If you want to build trust, both you and your employee need to have confidence in each other's decision-making skills.

Can you both count on the fact that you are who you say you are? If you have done the work in Habit One, this one will be apparent to both you and your people. People want to know that you are genuine and you stand for something that is significant. That is what they want from you and what you want from them.

How Do You Delegate?

Delegation, like everything else we talk about, is a process. People are typically turned off by the idea of delegation because at some time in the past they have had a bad experience. So, when starting this process you aren't going to announce that you are now delegating tasks, like you are Oprah handing out free cars. (You get a task, you get a task, you get a task!) My guess is that wouldn't go over great. Maybe you, or your employees, have had an experience where a task was delegated to someone else or someone delegated a task to them, and it fell flat on its face. It was an epic failure, and everyone ended up being the loser in the situation. The time and energy required to fix the problem took more time and energy than if they would have "just done it themselves" from the beginning. Most likely, the task didn't get delegated to someone, but instead was dumped on someone. There's a difference.

When you start considering delegating a task, it's important to recognize that delegation is a process. It takes time. There is no easy button or magic wand. To delegate, you must commit time and energy to making it successful. I know that sounds overwhelming, especially if you don't have time or energy to start with, but I promise you, it will be worth it.

To Delegate, You Need to Teach, Train, and Equip

To start, you need to teach values, the "why" of wanting a task done a certain way. To begin, you need to explain why this task is important. Let's say you are asking a parts support specialist to front and face the end caps in your showroom. You would teach them why you are doing this. As an example, you might say, "We want our customers to walk into our dealership and say 'WOW!'" or maybe, "We want the customer to have an effortless experience every time they walk in." The values you teach are going to be unique to your dealership and to the task, but you should identify and communicate clearly the "why" of what you are asking them to do.

Next, you need to train your employee on the "how," giving them skills they need to do the job.

If we go back to our example of fronting and facing the product on end caps, you would explain to the employee that in order to do this properly you would need to pull all of the products to the front of the shelf to make it look full, and then turn each item so that the labels are facing forward. I know it's not rocket science, but delegating is about teaching, not leaving things up to chance.

Now you have shown them specifically how you want this done. Then have them do the same task and provide clear and direct feedback. If you chose to skip this part of the teaching, you can't be upset with your people for not doing it right. You are the instructor; they are the inexperienced driver. Remember?

Finally, you need to equip the employee and give them the tools and authority to do the job. The last part can be the hardest, but it is also the most important. Ask your employee, "Are there any additional tools or supplies you need to do this task? Is there any authority you need to have to do this job?" Tools and authority. Ouch. Maybe in our hypothetical example, the person asks for a shop towel to make sure there are no fingerprints or oil smudges on the product.

In most cases, tools are typically easier to give than authority. But the authority to make the decisions on that particular task is as equally important.

In some situations, authority might be allowing them to decide when to do the task. If it's the example of fronting and facing shelves, you might want to instruct them to do it first thing every morning right when the dealership opens. Or you might give them the authority to decide to do it every day before lunch. You have to be okay with giving them the authority to decide when to do it if you want to take the task off your plate. I know, it's painful.

The most challenging part of delegating is that you must follow the 80 percent rule. The 80 percent rule is this: if someone does a task to 80 percent of how you would have done it, then it is good enough. That's right, 80 percent. Not 85 percent or 90 percent. Eighty percent has to be good enough. Let that sink in for a second. You might be thinking, "But Sara, there are certain things that require 100 percent accuracy. What about those?" You're right—taxes, counting the cash drawer, inventory management, payroll and repairs in the service department, and other similar tasks require a high degree of accuracy, but most everyday jobs can be done at 80 percent and still be acceptable.

I was at a dealer meeting recently, and we were talking about the 80 percent rule in delegation. A dealer came up to me after the session, trying to stump me, and said, "Sara, I have employees that set up our displays both in the store and in our outside display area. I am really particular about how they do them. Are you saying that I shouldn't be watching the cameras in the dealership and giving them feedback on what I want?"

I'm confident that my face showed my confusion before it came out of my mouth. I said, "That's exactly what I want you to do. If you have delegated them to do the task, then I am assuming that you have taught, trained, and equipped them to do it how you want it done. So, it's not something you need to be involved in." I told him, "This isn't easy, and I get that. But if you are involved in every small detail going on inside your dealership, you will never make any forward progress." What you will discover is that your employees will begin to take responsibility for the task, and, in the long run, will probably end up doing that task better than you ever did.

Giving your employees both the tools and authority are vital components of the delegation process. If you equip them with the tools, but not the authority, the task won't ever come off your plate and it will leave everyone involved, including yourself, frustrated.

Dumping a Task

One reason we all have such a terrible knee-jerk reaction to the topic of delegation is that we have either dumped a task on someone else or a task has been dumped on us. Either way, it's a defeating feeling that leaves both sides resigned to mediocrity.

When a task is dumped on an employee, this is what could happen: 1) "I need you to front and face the end caps." Employee is given the task. Then 2) "I can't believe you did such a terrible job." Employee is given feedback.

This leaves your employee being held responsible, when instead your goal should be for them to take responsibility.

How many of us have dumped a task on someone else? My guess is all of us. I've been there and I'm sure you have too.

Do you know when and where the most tasks are dumped in a dealership? When you are training a new employee. Consider this scenario. You hire a new parts person. For his training, you tell him to follow the parts manager who has worked for you for twenty years. Now, you don't want the new employee to pick up the bad habits or attitude of the veteran parts person, but you don't take the time to walk through teaching, training, or equipping the employee yourself. You ultimately end up frustrated when the new employee doesn't work out. The reason he didn't work out is because you dumped an entire job on him. You failed to teach, train, or equip him, which, in turn, caused him to fail.

If you want to be a master at utilizing the people in your dealership, you have to put the time and energy behind developing your skill of delegation.

Empowering Your People to Learn Doesn't Have to Be Expensive

Once we get this well-oiled delegation machine moving in the direction that allows you to take tasks off your plate, we don't get to collectively celebrate and move on. No, it's only the beginning. The moment when something moves from your plate to an employee's plate is when you should start investing in additional training.

When I bring up the topic of training employees, I find there are two distinct camps. The first group of dealers are all in. "Yes, train my people. And can I sit in the training too so that I can learn right along with them?" We call these people lifelong learners. In the other camp, you find dealers who get frustrated that their people weren't born knowing everything they needed to know about this specific task in the dealership. They assume the employee will pick up the knowledge by osmosis in their sleep (they won't). I don't know where you are at on the spectrum, but regardless, I do know that your people need training to continue to improve and grow.

A few years ago, we were working with a dealership outside of Cleveland, Ohio. This dealership, like many we work with, was in transition. The owner's daughter, Mary, was joining the business.

The dad, Jim, was committed to making sure that Mary was equipped to come in and perform at the same level as the rest of the employees. He decided to have her start as an inside salesperson, but she didn't have any sales experience. Jim was committed to making sure she not only had the skills she needed to be an excellent salesperson, but also wanted to make sure that, if she decided that the dealership was her long-term plan, she would have the skills necessary to run the dealership.

Over the next three years, Jim sent his daughter to sales training allowing her to learn and develop her sales skills. And that she did. Over those three years, she was regularly the top salesperson in the dealership. She was clearly excelling in the sales role. Jim then decided to take it a step further and have Mary attend management training classes that allowed her to understand the numbers coming out of each department and the processes that were needed to continue to make each department profitable. Through this process, Jim and Mary discovered that accounting was an obvious weakness and an area that she had never received training. Now, she really had no strong desire to be an accountant or bookkeeper, but because she wanted to one day run the business, she signed up for an intro to accounting course at the local community college.

Training your people should be focused not just on the skills they lack today, but on where you hope they go in the future. When you give your people the opportunity to learn, whether in a classroom or by letting them get their hands dirty and just trying, you are growing your people. Over time, you will maximize this valuable resource by allowing your people to learn and develop their skills. The result? Your dealership will be better for it and your plate will be a lot less heavy!

YOUR MANUFACTURERS

What's more of a challenge—asking your manufacturer for help or admitting to your mom that she was right, again? For many dealerships, the relationships with their manufacturers are strained ones. Some of these relationships are defined by frustration and need; while healthier ones are based on the premise that you both are trying to achieve the same thing, to sell a product, or to take care of the customer. Though I don't know all of the dynamics at play between you and your manufacturers, I do know that for most dealers your manufacturers and their teams are there to be a resource to you and help you be successful.

Your Suppliers Are on Your Team (Go Dealers!)

In order to understand how valuable of a resource a manufacturer or distributor can be for you, it might require thinking a little differently about what they bring to the table. Over the course of a month, how many people from your supplier's organization do you interact with? Who do you talk to, see, or email each month? More than a handful? Probably.

What if you viewed every representative from your manufacturer or distributor that you work with as a relationship to be developed and a resource to be utilized that can help you move your business forward? For many dealers and manufacturers, this shift in mindset is an important change that has to happen on both sides.

Not long ago, I was talking to a group of regional sales managers for a manufacturer we work with in Minnesota. One sales manager asked me, "What do dealers really need from us when we visit their dealership?" What a loaded question. At the heart of his question was his quest to make his dealers better and stronger and to be a valuable resource for them. We visited about the fact that under no circumstance was his visit more important than a customer of the dealership. We also talked about how he needed to be interested in the dealership, as a whole, and not solely focused on the sales order he was there to take from the owner or sales manager. One thing I mentioned really threw them for a loop. I told them that the most powerful tool that allows the dealer to understand that you are on their team is for you to act like it. When your salesperson goes into the dealership and the owner is busy with a customer, they should walk over to the literature rack, straighten it up, and load it back with new brochures.

Then walk back and talk to the service manager and see if they are struggling with any warranty issues that you might be able to help with. Find out from the parts manager if there are any parts they are struggling to get from you. Don't just hang out and drink coffee while you wait. Build relationships with the parts and service managers, which will undoubtedly improve the dealership.

Your manufacturer's "team" may include your salesperson, a regional salesperson, a service person, the technical troubleshooting team, the warranty team, and the marketing team, just to name a few. Use them, lean on them, and push each other to be better. Don't overlook the importance of these relationships. Instead, work to build them and make them stronger.

Often the best relationships are built during or after manufacturers and distributor dealer meetings. I know that some dealers don't take the time to attend these meetings, and sadly they are missing a great opportunity to build strong relationships with people who work for the manufacturer that outside of the meeting they will never get to know.

Those connections happen over lunch and dinner. Maybe you connect with a marketing person, a person who handles the warranty claims for the manufacturer, the one that oversees parts shipments to your dealership. When you are sitting around a table over dinner, sharing food and drink together, that's when the relationships between dealers are being built with the people on their manufacturer team. As a dealer, you have to commit to stepping away from your dealership and participating in these events whenever you can.

As I mentioned, the "we're on the same team" mentality is an important mindset shift for both sides, and when embraced by both the dealer and manufacturer, it allows everyone to move forward.

Your Manufacturers and Distributors Have Resources
They Are Begging You to Use (Please, Please, Please)

Let's talk about some of the ways vendors can come alongside you. Your suppliers work hard to provide quality programs that will help your dealership. The programs available to you are a result of many months of hard work of your manufacturer's and distributor's dealer development team, and other key departments. Their goal is not to overwhelm you, or cause you pain and suffering, but to help you be the best dealer you can be.

You may feel you need a PhD to understand how and when to utilize the programs that are rolled out each year. Sure, there are always a few "required" programs, but other offerings may either be suggested or just available to you. Your top priority is to be aware of the difference.

At the beginning of this chapter, Bob introduced you to Scott, who was a master at this. Not only did he make it a top priority to take advantage of the training they provided, he worked with his people to put it into place. With a little time and patience, and by making it a priority, you can work to identify which programs are required to achieve or maintain standards. Then, turn your attention to looking at other "available programs" that might be beneficial to you. Not every program that a manufacturer makes available will be a good fit for you. You read that right. You don't have to sign up for every manufacturer program that is available. Instead, work to find the ones that will give you an advantage and help you achieve your vision for the future. Take advantage of programs that are a good fit for you. In most cases there will be early order programs or preseason programs with free freight, extended payment terms, and extra discounts. Those programs are designed to help both you and the manufacturer. As much as possible, don't let those slide by you.

The second thing you must evaluate is the amount of time, energy, and money your participation in a program will require. Because you may have more than one major manufacturer, you must commit the time necessary to understand programs from each one or it will become a major challenge for even the most accomplished multitasker. Let's look at the three key questions you need to ask to see if a program is a fit for you.

HOW MUCH TIME IS THIS GOING TO TAKE?

From personal experience, we know that even if the program offered by the vendor is amazing, if you are not willing or able to invest the time to take advantage of it, it won't work for you. Often, a manufacturer will ask us to create a program that will help dealers apply and improve processes, and, when we do, we can count on one thing. The dealers who are successful with the programs go "all in" and get results. Those who do not commit fully, don't see the growth and success they had hoped for, leaving both the dealer and the manufacturer frustrated. Now, most programs don't require a lot of time up front, but they do require consistency. When a dealer says, "I just don't have time to do the work," we know that change will never happen.

Regardless of how great the program is, if you don't invest the time, nothing will change, and you will be in the same place tomorrow that you are today—still exhausted, but with less money in your pocket. Don't let that happen to you. If you want to see results, you have to fully commit to make the change. Be honest with yourself and your manufacturer. You can't commit to every program they have available at once and see results. Identify how much time you have and commit to making it work.

WHAT AMOUNT OF ENERGY WILL BE REQUIRED FOR THIS TO BE SUCCESSFUL?

If you make the decision to engage and fully utilize a program, what amount of energy will you need to invest? One manufacturer we work with has a marketing program that helps dealers by creating websites and helping to keep them updated. It takes a significant amount of upfront effort to get a website up and ready for your team to upload information and maintain the site. With the help of the manufacturer's and distributor's marketing team, the amount of attention you have to give is much less compared to if you were to do this on your own. Consider reaching out to your suppliers for tasks you are not an expert on and that require a lot more attention from you and your people. The more you can allow the manufacturer to assist with areas that are not your strengths, the more you will be freed up to focus on and maximize the other resources in your dealership.

HOW MUCH MONEY WILL I NEED TO INVEST?

Let's talk about the money that you work so hard to put into your bank account. One thing we see successful dealers do is create a budget, before the programs become available, and stick to the budget! Now, I understand there are three types of people who, when reading the word *budget*, have a strong reaction. The first person reacts with, "NO! NOT A BUDGET!" A second person will say, "I've tried a budget before, and it just didn't work for me." And the third happily reacts with, "I love a good budget!" I'm not sure where you are on this continuum, but what I do know is that a budget gives you permission to spend money in your dealership. It also gives you the unprecedented ability to say no, and the ability to blame the no on the budget.

As we sit, I can't tell you exactly what amount or percentage of your budget should go to additional programs and outside resources, because there are a lot of different factors to consider. Things like the size of your dealership, the number of employees you have and their willingness to participate, as well as your margins and your pain points all impact how much money you should set aside each year. Some of the most common outside resources that are often included in this budget item include training, marketing services (not your actual marketing costs), communication services, signage, and any other special programs that your manufacturer rolls out. Your budget for programs and outside resources will be different from the dealership down the street, and it may take some time to get it right. But when you find that program that allows you to maximize your dollars and time, you have hit the jackpot!

Maximizing Your Marketing Money

One of the most underutilized resources that manufacturers make available for dealers is the humble co-op dollar. Remember when Bob told you that Scott not only uses all his co-op funds but isn't afraid to ask for more? Sadly, a lot of co-op money goes unused by the other dealers.

When we start talking about marketing, marketing budgets, and co-op dollars, many times dealers look at us like we have started speaking a foreign language. I get it, it can be a lot. But let me break this down, specifically as it relates to using your co-op dollars to help you reach your goals.

It's clear that most dealers don't wake up every morning and say, "I can't wait to dive into the dealership's marketing strategy today!" No, most dealerships view marketing as a necessary evil. They know they need to spend money on marketing to increase their sales, but they don't even know where to start. Maybe you feel like this; investing in marketing is like burying money in the ground, with the hope that it grows roots and magically produces huge amounts of sales.

So, how much should you spend?

You don't need an advanced math degree to figure out how much you should spend on marketing. In fact, you can figure it out with just a little information and a few numbers that should be right at your fingertips.

When planning your marketing budget, most dealerships fall into the 5 percent or the 3 percent category.

THE 5 PERCENT CATEGORY

If you have been in business for five years or less, or if you have brought on a new major line in the last five years, you should invest 5 percent of your gross revenue on marketing. That means 5 percent of all money generated from every department in your dealership. For the sake of easy math, if you were a million-dollar dealer in the 5 percent category, you would have a marketing budget of $50,000.

THE 3 PERCENT CATEGORY

If you are a dealership who has been in business for more than five years and have not brought on a new major line in the last five years, you would be in the 3 percent category. Meaning, if you did a million dollars of gross revenue per year in your dealership you would have a marketing budget of $30,000. You may think that's a lot of money, and you would be right. But, when you look at this number, keep in mind that not all of that money should come directly out of your pocket.

Your goal is to have at least half your marketing co-oped by your manufacturers. To best maximize those precious dollars, you will need to have a plan for the money (or a budget!!). Your manufacturers will have lots of options to help you with your marketing. Some will allow you to use it for an open house; some will allow it to be used for outside signage and inside displays.

Most manufacturers have entire teams of people who specialize in marketing, and they have an extensive amount of data to back up what is working best for your target customer. The act of reaching out and asking for help will go a long way in maximizing your co-op money.

We don't expect you to be an expert in marketing. We expect you to be an expert on your business. The perk you have is that many of the strong manufacturers you work with have experts in marketing and can help you create a plan that is right for you.

As you learn about new programs, I encourage you to do a gut check and ask yourself, "Do I have the time (or can I make the time), will this get the energy it deserves, and do I have the money to make it successful?" If the answer to all three is yes, go fully into the program that your manufacturer has made available for you.

Your Manufacturers and Distributors Want (No, Need) You to Be Successful

A few years ago, I was at a dealer meeting listening to a panel of CEOs from a few major agriculture manufacturers. They spent an hour talking about how they saw their companies adapting in the future and the role the servicing dealer would play. At the end of the panel, the moderator asked the panelists how they could best help their dealers be successful. One said that he had made changes in his organization so that his employees would start looking at their dealers as their customers instead of the end user. He viewed his dealers as customers, and his organization was willing to do whatever it took to keep his customers satisfied. Something about this struck me as off, but it wasn't until a few months later that I realized what it was.

A few months later, I was visiting with the president of a major manufacturer. During our conversation he offhandedly mentioned he viewed his dealers as partners. Intrigued, I asked why that was. He told me that their business was nothing without the dealers who sold and serviced their products. Partners are in for the long haul, but with customers it's a transactional relationship. That was it, and that was why this manufacturer was adored by its dealers. I asked him how he communicated this to the other people in the organization, and he said, "Well, it's relatively simple. If they don't take care of the dealers, they won't have a job." Without the dealers, the manufacturer couldn't succeed, and the dealers needed the manufacturer in the same way.

When we shift from a customer and supplier mentality to a partner mentality, something fundamentally changes. Both parties are concerned about the other's success, and their actions reflect that.

Now, I'm not so naive to think this is how every manufacturer/ dealer relationship operates, but I do know there are good manufacturers who care deeply about their dealer base and are doing whatever it takes for them to succeed.

For a manufacturer or distributor, finding a dealer to carry their brand and getting them set up to be successful is the equivalent of you trying to find a good A-level technician who understands the intricacy of your product mix and has the training needed to get started right away. It's not an easy task. Manufacturers and distributors spend a lot of money to bring on a new dealer, and for most of them they are committed to seeing that dealer succeed. Do you know what costs more than bringing on a new dealer for most of your vendors? Closing a dealer. Your manufacturers and distributors need you to be successful. They need you to be a force in the marketplace. They need you to push the envelope and help them understand how they can better partner with you. They can't read your mind. They aren't in your dealership every day. The only way that they know how to partner with you more effectively is if you tell them.

One dealer we were working with was recently invited to be on the dealer council for one of the lines she carries. She decided to accept. I asked her why she had chosen to invest her time this way. She said, "The only way that the manufacturers can get better is if I make the time and help." Try as your manufacturers may, the only way they can get better at partnering with you and help you achieve success is if you tell them what is and what isn't working. Unfortunately (or fortunately in some situations) they don't have a crystal ball and they can't read your mind. The only way they know when something is or isn't working at the dealership level is when you tell them. As in any partnership, that takes time, energy, and communication. Both you and your manufacturer can get better and achieve success as you move from a customer mentality to a partner mentality.

THE POWER OF OTHERS

What if the task you need off your plate is more complex than something you can delegate to an employee or perhaps more niche than what your vendors can help with? It could be an overwhelming legal problem. Maybe you have gotten to a place with your business that you are showing a profit, but your bank account doesn't reflect it (more on that later). Or what if you have to make the hard decision of letting someone on your team go? Where do you turn in situations like these?

No matter what you are facing, the most important thing you can do is be humble enough to ask for help. It's okay that you don't have all the answers. Your people will not think less of you because you asked for some assistance. I promise, they won't. What they will see is a leader who is willing to admit they don't have all the answers and is strong enough to seek them.

The Dealers Around You (Let's All Be Friends)

There is something powerful about National Dealer Meetings, live training events, and trade shows. First, these environments have a special energy. Maybe it's the result of playing "The Eye of the Tiger" for the fifteenth time, but more likely because you are surrounded by people who are all striving to develop and grow their businesses. But the other powerful component of these events is that dealers realize they aren't in the battle alone. There are other dealers who are walking through the same challenges as you are, or who have dealt with them in the past and have come out the other side. There is something powerful about knowing you aren't alone.

A few years ago, we were working with a manufacturer on a program that focused on taking highly motivated dealers and helping them move their business to the next level. Each year, this group of dealers met the day before the national dealer meeting to continue to learn and connect with each other. One year, just prior to the meeting, one of those dealers was hit from all sides. The worst part, he was dealing with a major theft issue involving a family member. It goes without saying, this took a huge toll on him, his family, his finances, and his entire dealership. He had been an active part of this group, and when he shared his story and struggles, he was met with encouragement and support. In that moment, he was not alone. He was around other people who understood the risk, the exhaustion, and the pressure, and they were willing to come alongside and hold him up in the midst of it.

Connecting with dealers can provide you with other benefits. By adopting a "smarter not harder" approach we see dealers partnering with other non-competing dealers. I know of one group of non-competing dealers who plan their marketing together and share a graphic designer to help minimize cost and time. Another group meets regularly to talk about safety in their dealership, each offering different safety training based on what they are learning. Still another group meets for accountability on their projections and budgets. Regardless of what you need, other like-minded dealers can be an invaluable resource.

Take the initiative and reach out to other dealers and begin to develop relationships. Find a group or groups where you can seek advice or direction. Now, it might feel a little like going on a first date at the beginning, but push through that awkwardness and be open to sharing your journey. This doesn't have to be an overly complex process. Take the step to make some new connections that will allow you to find new resources and be a resource to others.

Who's Your Coach?

Have you ever gotten in over your head? Ha! How about today? Probably. Most business owners, like you, are entrepreneurs to their core. What does that mean? An entrepreneur will do whatever it takes to find a solution to a problem. You can do it yourself, except when you can't. As painful as it might be, the resource of other experts is a powerful tool.

When I was in high school, I was a competitive swimmer, which basically means my mom or dad got up at 4 a.m. every morning to take me to swim practice (thanks Mom and Dad!). My favorite event? The mile. That's right. I wasn't fast, but I could just keep swimming, and swimming, swimming, swimming, swimming, like no one else. Plus, I hated to lose. Now, there were times I lost a race, but I never quit. In my mind, quitting was the equivalent of losing, and I was never going to quit.

I couldn't control how much the other swimmers practiced, or if they were born with genetics that allowed them to be a water torpedo (I wasn't). I could control how often I practiced, my attitude at practice, and the effort I put in. I also knew that if I wanted to get better, I needed other resources. I needed a coach who could push me to be better. I needed swim gear (I think I owned over twenty pairs of goggles), and I needed access to a pool. Without those resources, I wouldn't have had the ability to get better.

The resources you need in your dealership are not a pool or a pair of goggles but, instead, an expert or advisor who can coach and walk alongside you in the areas of business that are not your strength.

Here are a few sources where you can find a coach or outside advisor.

DEALER ASSOCIATIONS

Your national and local dealer associations are an incredible wealth of knowledge on the everchanging landscape of rules and legislation in your industry. The people who run these associations are the ones who go into battle for your industry, working to make sure state and federal legislation provides positive outcomes for dealers. They work to develop, alongside manufacturers, cutting-edge apprenticeship programs and technical training. They are also working to keep their members updated on current industry trends that might affect dealerships. So, unless you feel like you have the time and energy to keep track of all of those items, while running your dealership, you should consider joining your local association and allow them to be part of your team. The small investment you make will pay out in big dividends for you and your fellow dealers.

BUSINESS PROFESSIONAL TEAM

Your team of business professionals includes people like your banker, attorney, CPA, and insurance agent. It doesn't take much to be overwhelmed by the minute details of taxes and insurance. These members of your team can help ensure that you are meeting all of your legal requirements and safeguarding your business assets against loss or liability.

Maybe you are like one of our dealers who has an attorney on his team who specializes in succession planning. This dealership, who is just beginning the process of transitioning the business from the first generation to the second, meets at least once a year with this advisor/attorney who leads their family through all of the hard and uncomfortable conversations, makes sure that everyone is still going in the same direction, and provides a neutral perspective on this incredibly tense and emotional topic. Bring your business team together at least a couple of times each year. You want your banker, your CPA, your insurance agent, and your attorney all in the same room so each knows what the other is trying to help you with. You will benefit from them all being on the same page that you are on.

Resources That Keep You Learning and Growing

The resources you use to move your business forward don't always have to be complex. Maybe you are seeking a solution to a specific problem and you decide to pick up a book. I know, if you are reading this, it's clear that you don't have a deep-seeded fear of books (way to go!). So why not order another one? Need something on managing cash flow? Are you struggling with time management? Have a desire to gain a better understanding of your customers? Marketing maybe? There is an ever-growing list of great books and resources available that can help you move each department forward. On our website, we have a plethora of free blogs available to help get you started on almost anything you might encounter in your dealership. Couple that with webinars and resources available from your manufacturers, and you have the world at your fingertips, but it's up to you to make the decision to use them.

Remember, many companies like ours spend every day working with dealers, troubleshooting the issues they run into, and sharing best practices. There is nothing you are dealing with that would shock us. I promise. We have heard and seen just about everything.

Did you just move all your retirement savings into the business to keep the doors open? We won't judge you, and we can help. Has the transition of the business from one generation to the next left the family completely divided and now no one is speaking to each other? We are so sorry. Is your parts person dating another employee, and it makes things weird for everyone else? We have walked through it.

Sometimes, in these overwhelming moments, it can be hard to figure out what your next step should be, and a coach or an advisor can be a phenomenal resource to help you see your blind spots and work with you to create a plan to move forward.

Successful dealers, who apply and utilize their resources, don't necessarily have all the answers. But they have spent the time and energy developing relationships with people who are experts in their field. They never stop learning, and above all they never quit. Use your resources and develop strong relationships. Look for partnerships and opportunities that allow you to work with people who have your best interests at heart.

HABIT FOUR:

Know and Understand
the Numbers

I'M THE PROBLEM: *Numbers shumbers—
they take care of themselves.*
I'M THE SOLUTION: *Numbers don't lie.*

It was almost December when my team and I had our first web-cast with Ron and his son Kyle. They had just joined one of our groups and were giving us an overview of their dealership, its history, their people, and what they hoped to accomplish over the next twelve months. Ron had a small dealership with six employees, including Kyle. They were seeing growth and excited about their future and the upcoming season.

As we began the meeting, I asked them to share what they hoped to gain by working with us. Kyle was the first to speak. "We want to make more money. We are growing, but the business is costing more to run. Plus, we are not able to take out much personally in the way of salary." Ron added, "Bob, we touch a lot of money; we are just not good at keeping it." We all laughed because, sadly, it was a familiar story.

Far too many dealers know how to make money; they just don't know how to keep it. As we talked, my team and I shared with them the critical numbers they needed to understand and the importance of monitoring them on a daily, weekly, and monthly basis. "The key to being profitable in any business, whether it is a dealership like you have or a grocery store, is to know what the critical numbers are and manage to them," we told them.

Their BCI advisor added, "That means, for both of you, you are going to become friends with the reports your software produces over the next twelve months and we will show you how to manage to them. Everything in a dealership has a number attached to it, whether it's your people, your marketing, your expenses, or sales of product, parts, service, or rentals. And everything with a number can be managed. We can show you the numbers you need to work toward. Numbers that will make you profitable."

There was a pause before Kyle said, "I'm not good with numbers." I laughed and said, "Your software is good with numbers, I just need you to be able to read." They laughed and let me know that they both could not only read but write! "We'll start by helping you find your current numbers," I continued, "and work with you to manage the difference between those numbers and where you want to go."

That was the beginning of our journey with Ron and Kyle. It has been almost four years since our first meeting. Since that time, they have both become number ninjas. They live and breathe the reports from their software and, two years ago, began taking 7 percent of every dollar of profit and depositing it in a separate checking account. They are working toward building their own credit line. There is no doubt in my mind that they won't make it happen.

It is better to be a $1 million dealer who keeps $150,000 than a $6 million dealer who loses money. A common misconception is that if you touch a lot of money, you are a healthy dealer, but that couldn't be further from the truth. Let's have Sara share an example with you.

. . .

Bob is right. We know a dealer who sells $5 million of outdoor power equipment each year. That is a lot of lawn mowers! This dealer typically wins annual awards at national manufacturer meetings, qualifies for incentive trips, and is looked at as an example for other dealers. However, at the end of last year, he was forced to take a deep dive into his line of credit just to keep the doors open and bills paid.

In comparison, a dealer we work with sells approximately $1 million of outdoor power equipment each year. (That's still a lot of lawn mowers!) Sadly, this dealer hasn't qualified for any incentive trips and doesn't win major awards at the national dealer meetings. However, at the end of this past year, he was able to put $150,000 in his pocket! He monitors his numbers, keeps his eye daily on his cash flow, and adjusts his overall operation throughout the year based upon those numbers. The result? He achieved a dream and completed a purchase of a vacation home in Florida for his family!

Which is the more successful dealer?

So often, people assume the quantity of money that a dealership touches over the course of time is what determines success. In reality, the amount of money a dealer is able to keep at the end of the day is what makes a successful, and profitable, dealer.

What differentiates the profitable $1 million dealer from the $6 million dealer who is losing money?

The profitable dealer:

1. Lives and breathes his numbers.
2. Takes his profit first.
3. Utilizes salary caps for every department.

Let's dive into each of these individually so we can help you keep more of the money you are touching.

To understand your business is to understand your numbers. You will never truly have control of your business until you have a firm grasp on how to track the numbers and understand the cause and effect of each number, and what you can do to influence it.

If you are like most dealers, your problem isn't that you don't have access to your numbers but, instead, you are drowning in the data that is coming out of your dealership and you don't have the time, knowledge, or energy to make sense of it.

I understand that most of you didn't start your dealership because you love numbers; however, if your focus is to be profitable, the numbers in your dealership must become like another language that you speak fluently. This language is something you will need to teach the rest of your team. Then, you will need to consistently communicate with your managers using the language of numbers. You don't want to get rusty and forget it. Oui?

While different industries may have different names for these key performance indicators (KPIs), the purpose of all numbers are the same. They allow you to get a quick read on the health of your dealership, and its departments, by simply looking at a number.

One last note before we dive in. I want to make sure we are all on the same page (literally and figuratively) about the best way to use this section. Some of you may need a drink to get through this chapter because you "aren't numbers people." I see you, and I support whatever you need in order to tackle this subject. My personal drink choice is a Diet Coke, but make your own decisions. You will also need a calculator. The one on your phone will work just fine because, despite what your sixth-grade math teacher said about learning to do math in your head because "you won't always have a calculator with you," you will always have a calculator with you.

I want you to start with just one department and calculate the numbers for that department. I know, some of you have the tendency to be overachievers and want to jump into all of the numbers for all of the departments at the same time. We know, you were in AP calculus and we feel your judgment. But, for now, just take it slow. You will not be able to change everything at one time, so start with the department that is the least profitable (cough, probably service, cough) and work on those first. You don't get a high-five or gold star for trying to change everything today. What do you get if you try to do it all at one time? Overwhelmed and frustrated employees. We'll start by focusing on one area—service. I promise the other pages will still be here when you are ready for them.

Top Three Service Department Numbers:

Recovery Rate for Department = Total Billed Hours / Total Paid Hours

Your shop or service department's recovery rate tells you what percentage of time you are buying each day (eight hours per technician) compared to the amount of time that you are selling each day.

This number tells us a few very important things. First, it gives you a cohesive view of the amount of work coming into the service department. If you have a recovery rate below 80 percent, you need to start putting more effort into improving your processes or marketing the service department to ensure a steady stream of work is coming in. The responsibility to maintain a consistent flow of work coming into the service department is the job of the service manager, if you have one.

Second, your recovery rate allows you to see if you are going to need another technician soon. I know, you always feel like you need another technician, but keep in mind we run a dealership based on what the numbers tell us, not how we feel. If you aren't selling all of the time you currently have available, or using the inventory you are currently buying each day, you need better processes, not another person. Once you get to the point where your recovery rate for the department is in the 90-95 percent range, then you will need to look for another technician. It is an indicator that your service department is almost at capacity.

Tech Efficiency =
Billed Hours / Actual Time Clocked On the Work Order

Technician efficiency tells you, by technician, how quickly a job is completed versus what the service department was able to charge for it. When tech efficiency is less than 85 percent, you will know that a technician was given a service or repair he or she was not equipped for, or the job was underpriced for the complexity of the job. This might mean that the technician needed additional training, or additional resources such as different tools, or that the service manager or writer needs to change their pricing strategy.

Tech efficiency should be monitored daily by the service manager or service writer. An "A" level tech should consistently beat the time set for a job by at least 20 percent. A "B" level tech should be able to hit the time allowed for the service or repair. If that is not happening, there is a problem with job pricing.

In the dealerships we work with, there are a large number of technicians who are consistently over 100 percent efficient. Here is how you determine a tech's efficiency. Let's say you billed out nine hours and the technician was clocked onto work orders for eight hours. In this case your technician would be 112 percent efficient. We see this and higher numbers every single day from shops all over the country. If it's possible in one dealership, then it's possible in your dealership. This is typically achieved by flat rating, utilizing menu pricing, and resisting the urge to put your best technician on time and material jobs (seriously, this is a terrible idea, if you are not multiplying the time by their efficiency!).

If you notice this number starting to go down, again, it should be a warning (like your smoke detector battery beeping at 3:00 a.m.) that the technician doesn't have the training or resources to do the job.

Average Completion Time for Shop = Total Completed Work Orders / Total Actual Time

Another number you want to monitor monthly is your average completion time. The average completion time for the shop tells your service manager how far booked ahead his department is.

All customers have the same question: "When can I get this back?" Now, if you are like most of the dealerships we work with, they would take a look at their lot, take a quick guess, and say, "We'll have it back to you soon," which is about as unclear and non-committal as telling someone you'd like to grab lunch soon. However, if you are tracking your average shop completion time, you can give them a very good estimate. For example, let's say you have a customer bring in a unit for repair and there are twenty-five work orders in front of them. From your numbers you would know that during the last week your three technicians were able to complete one hundred repairs in the combined 120 hours they were in the service department. In this case, you can let the customer know they can expect to have their unit back in approximately two days. This number alone will reduce frustration for you and your customers too!

There are a multitude of other numbers that you can look at in your service department. However, if you are trying to make sense of the constant stream (or lack thereof) of information coming out of your service department, the three numbers we just reviewed will allow you to take an objective look at how your service department is doing. Let's be honest. After you pull the numbers, it might be a little painful, like root canal painful or even your in-laws staying at your house for all of Christmas break painful, but that is how you make progress. But if you continue keeping your head in the sand, then that means *you* are the problem! However, you now have the solution in your hands. Begin today and take a look at the cold, hard numbers of your service department. Want more? For you overachiever types, we have added a full list of key performance indicators (KPIs) in the appendix of this book.

Remember Ron and Kyle from the beginning of this chapter who had become number ninjas? They told us that a daily check of their shop numbers is like monitoring the instrument gauges in their trucks. It tells them, immediately, if their processes and people are functioning at the highest level of performance possible. Each day, they print out the reports they need and can quickly complete a diagnostic on the overall health of the department. They have seen an incredible turnaround, and the service department is now their largest producer of net profit.

Now, let's take a look at three of the parts department numbers you should be monitoring.

Fill Rate Out of Stocking Inventory = Total Parts Sold – Lost Sales, Special Orders, and Emergency Orders / Total Parts Sold Goal: 85 percent to 90 percent

Your fill rate out of stocking inventory tells you what percentage of the time you are able to fulfill the customers' order the first time they come in for a specific part.

The struggle is that often you don't have the information necessary to calculate this number. Specifically, if you are like most of the dealers we work with, you don't keep track of your lost sales. Lost sales are simply the sales you were not able to fulfill because the part was not in stock. Most parts people let the customer walk out the door and never take time to note the request for the part, usually because they are busy helping the next customer in line. However, if you want to have the parts the customer needs when they walk in, you must put a process in place to get this information.

Your special orders (parts you have to order because that particular part is not routinely stocked) and your emergency orders (the parts your service department or customer needs the next day regardless of the cost) are all factored into this equation.

Your goal is to have a fill rate out of stocking inventory between 85 and 90 percent. This is what you expect of most of your manufacturers, so it only makes sense that your customers can expect it of you. What do you call a person who expects others to perform at a higher standard than they themselves do? A hypocrite. Don't be a parts department hypocrite.

I recently had a dealer who said he disagreed and wanted to have his higher than 95 percent. I said, "Listen, if you have all the money in the world, and all the space, you can go for 100 percent, but for most dealers it's just not realistic to get much higher than 90 percent."

How do you improve your fill rate out of stocking inventory? The key is to have a wide but shallow parts inventory. This means you need a plan for inventory minimums and maximums that is connected to demand. Again, you need to keep track of lost parts sales to understand the demand. Most of the dealers we work with will start stocking a part when there are three unique demands over the course of a year, and they will start phasing out the part when there are less than two demands over that same period of time.

Your ultimate goal is to have a small quantity of the majority of the parts you need in stock, while not increasing your investment in your parts inventory. How can you do this? Well, these days, most manufacturers can get you parts within forty-eight hours, if need be.

Average Transaction Time = Start-to-Finish Time with a Counter Customer

The average transaction time, simply put, is a measurement of how long it takes a customer to walk up to the parts counter, get their part, pay, and be on their merry way. Most owners and managers have never taken the time to look at this number; however, a lower number typically means a better customer experience.

If this is the first time for you to track this number, you will probably be somewhere between twelve and fifteen minutes. Your goal is to be as close to twelve minutes as possible. It looks like this. The customer walks up to the parts counter and describes the part they need, the part is pulled and paid for, and the customer leaves—all within twelve minutes.

Think about a time when a torrent of customers came into your dealership and walked up to the parts counter. Put yourself in their shoes for just a moment. Specifically, think about the fifth person in line. A fifteen-minute transaction time isn't a huge issue when you are the first one in line. But when you are number five in line, and there are only two parts counter people and you end up waiting over thirty minutes to get the part you need, well, now you have a group of frustrated customers on your hands that could rival a group of moms waiting for Target to open on Black Friday. Your goal is to get the average transaction time down to twelve minutes or less per customer.

To measure your average transaction time, use a stopwatch or your phone and time how long it takes for your parts people to assist a line of customers. Then, divide the time by the number of people served. Do this a few times throughout a week and then average them out. Some owners or parts managers will measure the time using cameras in their dealership. That way the parts people don't know they are being timed and you will generate a more accurate number.

You have the power (yep, you are the solution) to decrease the average transaction time by making a few simple changes. First, make sure your fastest-moving parts are as close to the parts counter as possible.

You should also consider allowing customers to look up their own parts by providing a terminal for them to use. Now, before you start throwing bricks, shoes, or tomatoes in my direction, hear me out. The people who walk into your dealership have been taught by other retailers how to look up items themselves. Haven't you ever complained that customers are already looking up their parts online? Come on, we know you have. So, why not equip them to look up the parts they need and give them the ability to pull from the fifty fastest-moving parts. I'm sure you have a laundry list of reasons that this "won't work for your dealership," but we have dealers around the country who are having great success with this approach, while creating a better customer experience and decreasing transaction time.

A third option to consider is this. If you have the capacity, have your parts support specialist handle the transaction and check out customers, while the parts person looks up parts. Similar to a restaurant where you place your order here and pay and pick up your order there. This is a great way to improve your parts counter process.

And finally, the simplest, but often most challenging way to reduce transaction time? Remove the stools in front of and behind the parts counter. I can hear the collective groan as I mention this. "NO! Not the stools!" While this is not something that has to happen year-round, during season there shouldn't be a row of stools available on either side of the counter. This change will allow you to decrease transaction time, in an easy, low-cost way.

Parts Margins

Let's talk about margins. We talked about this briefly in Habit 2 but it's worth diving deeper. A few years ago I was having dinner at a national dealer meeting, and the person sitting next to me, who had been in business for about three years, said, "Until you mentioned it in your session today, I never knew I could mark my parts margins up over MSRP." I think my jaw hit the floor, and if it didn't my face said exactly what I was thinking. I don't know who needs to hear this, but your margins do not have to be set at MSRP. MSRP stands for Manufacturer SUGGESTED Retail Price. (Please note the word SUGGESTED!)

All manufacturers have a formula to help them create what they deem to be a competitive MRSP, based on the wholesale cost that you paid for the part and what they consider to be a fair margin for you. While it is important from a manufacturer's side to have consistent pricing on the same part throughout their dealer channel, in reality, depending on where your dealership is located it may cost more to run your dealership in your region than someone with the exact same lines in a different region of the country. Because of that, as I mentioned before, MSRP is just a suggestion. It's up to you to determine if the manufacturer's suggestion is correct for your situation. If you have a part that turns four or more times a year, then MSRP is probably going to be about right for that part. On the other hand, if it turns less than four times, you will need a higher margin to offset your lack of turns. Having some of your parts above MSRP is not something to feel guilty about, but it is something you have to focus on.

Now, as I mentioned before, this is more of an art form. There are some items that almost every customer has a good idea of what the price should be. For those parts, you should price them at (or even a little below) MSRP. For parts they don't have any idea of what the price should be, you will want to have higher margins to make up the difference.

Take a moment to look at your current parts margins and do two things:

1. IDENTIFY WHERE YOUR PARTS MARGINS ARE CURRENTLY SET.

While every industry is different, your goal should be to average a minimum of 8 percent over your MSRP. Most of the dealers we work with have their parts margins set at 38-42 percent at minimum (excluding parts sold to service for warranty). We have a group of dealers who are a bit more aggressive and closer to that 42-48 percent range. And we have some who are completely insane (just kidding) that run in the 48 percent range and higher. The first thing to do is determine where you are at currently in order to gauge where you are heading.

2. CALCULATE WHAT FINANCIAL GAIN YOU WOULD EXPERIENCE IF YOU WERE TO INCREASE YOUR MARGINS BY 3 PERCENT.

My guess is it would be a significant amount of money, and that money would be net profit, meaning all expenses have been paid on it, so it would go in your pocket. Please feel free to celebrate this with a cheer, smile, or even an ice cream cone.

Start by adjusting your margins on some of the slow-moving items in your inventory. Then, begin to work on a long-term plan to slowly increase the margins on your parts.

If you want to dive into more numbers, because you feel like you could recite the three above in your sleep, there are more in the appendix and on our free resources quick link at bobclements.com.

. . .

It's time to focus on how you can become the solution (and not the problem) in sales. This is an area where you must be vigilant. It is too easy to just let the sales department slide. Sales is not as tangible as parts and service and often gets a pass on managing the department like you should. Don't let those smooth-talking salespeople convince you otherwise. Sales has KPIs too, and you need to understand and monitor them regularly.

Here are the three sales department numbers you should always know, for each salesperson.

Average Sales per Salesperson = Total Sales / Number of Salespeople

Hitting projected sales goals is critical to the health of the dealership. Without reaching the levels they anticipate, many dealers struggle to maintain profit to cover dealership expenses. Knowing the average number of sales per salesperson will help you and your team set daily activity goals. These goals will also allow you to evaluate your salespeople against the average, to determine who on your team might be struggling and needs additional training.

Touches per Salesperson = Minimum of Twenty per Day

While I talked about this briefly in Habit Two, I wanted to go a little more in depth.

A question I hear often is, "How do I make sure we have success in sales?" The answer has to do with activity or, specifically, the number of touches your salespeople have daily.

A customer touch can be any interaction that your salesperson has with a customer. This could be a phone call, an email, a text, a minivan full of people who ask to use the bathroom, or even a walk-in customer; these would all count as customer touches.

When we are working with dealerships, we typically tie a salesperson's base pay to the number of touches they are willing to make each day. The minimum level that we allow an inside salesperson to commit to is twenty touches a day. We then require our salespeople to keep track of the number of touches by day. If your salesperson or salespeople play the "You can't make me keep track" card, it's clear they are not going to fit where you are going as a dealership. You can either change the people or you can change the people. Meaning, you can either encourage personal change, or you need to put a new person in the position. Regardless, letting someone hold you hostage in your business is not an option.

Closing Ratio = Customer Quotes / Sales Transactions

Looking at the closing ratio in sales is the salesperson's equivalent to the batting average for a professional baseball team (go Royals!).

Our goal is that salespeople having a closing ratio of around 40 percent. What this means is that of the contacts (qualified prospects who are provided a quote and have the ability to purchase) who walk into the dealership, 40 percent of them end up buying from you.

If the percentage is below 40 percent, there could be a few factors at play. Perhaps the salesperson isn't following the sales process, asking for the sale, or even qualifying the customer, to find out if the prospect has the means to buy before spending their valuable time with them.

What's the best part about knowing your current closing ratios? These percentages can easily be improved with training and practice. You and I both know that no baseball player would step up to the plate for the first time and assume they will have a .400 season. For a professional baseball player to achieve a .400 season, they must invest hours of hard work and practice, then maintain that intense focus all season. If you want your salespeople to consider themselves professionals and to improve their closing ratios, they will need training and coaching along the way.

Now before you get swept away in the excitement of pulling the numbers of these three departments, you must also take time to evaluate the health of other important areas of your dealership.

This is no different than going to the doctor for a checkup. When you arrive for your appointment, the doctor doesn't just take your blood pressure and declare you healthy. Instead, they also take your temperature, your weight (yikes!), and your pulse. All of these separate measurements (or numbers) together gives the doctor a cohesive view of your health, and the same can be said about your dealership. You have to look at the dealership's financial statements, cash flow, marketing ROI, department numbers, and salary caps to fully understand the health of your dealership.

MARKETING DEPARTMENT NUMBERS

In the last chapter we visited briefly about marketing in your dealership. You learned that hope isn't a marketing strategy that will work. Hope won't sprout magical money tree roots and send a drove of customers with small unmarked bills in your direction.

You can measure what's happening as a result of your marketing, just like any other department, and you should. However, marketing numbers are often some of the most overlooked numbers. If I were to give you only two numbers to look at in regard to marketing, they would be your customer acquisition cost and your customer lifetime value. Two numbers . . . you can handle that.

Customer Acquisition Cost =
Marketing Dollars Spent / New Customers

The customer acquisition cost tells you how much it costs to "buy" a new customer or to have a new customer come through your doors and make their first purchase from your dealership. To calculate this number, you will need to know two things.

1. How much was spent on marketing over a specific period of time
2. The number of new customers who bought from you over that same period of time

Now, if all your employees meticulously keep notes in a CRM, entering the information of each new customer, adding tags and notes to each new entry, making it easy to identify all your newest customers, then this is an easy number to track. It isn't lost on me that, for most dealerships, that scenario is what dreams are made of. If you do have people maintaining records like that, do a happy dance and give everyone in your dealership a high-five, because you all deserve it. However, if this isn't the case, all hope is not lost. You will still be able to calculate this number; it will just take a little more work.

If you don't have this information, start the process by focusing on the next seven days. I want you to account for all of the marketing money you spend over the next seven days and the number of new customers who buy from you during that time frame. Let's say, for example, you haven't been tracking these numbers. You decide to do a big sale, and you spend money on direct mail pieces, graphic design, postage, and labels. You would take the cost of those items, then look at the number of people who bought from you once the mailer was sent out. Will that give you a cohesive picture of your customer acquisition cost? Nope. Will it give you a starting point? You bet.

If this is your first time looking at this number, it may not mean a lot, but as you continue to monitor it month after month, it will allow you to see how well your marketing is paying off in the long run.

Here is how this will work: Let's say you run a new ad, and before the ad was ran, your customer acquisition cost was twenty-six dollars. After the ad, you recalculate your customer acquisition cost and see that it is now twenty-four dollars. What would that tell you? That your marketing is working. Now, on the flip side, if this number moved up to twenty-seven dollars, it would indicate that the ad you ran was not as effective as you had hoped.

Customer Lifetime Value =
Number of Customers / Revenue × Lifetime

The customer lifetime value (CLV) provides an estimate of how much income each customer will generate for you over the course of their lifetime as your customer. You need a few pieces of information to calculate the CLV. First, you need the total number of customers who have purchased from you over a set period of time (one year is the best, but work with what you have). You can break this down by department or look at it as a dealership as a whole. If you're just getting started, it will be easiest to look at the whole dealership, and you can nerd out on the specific numbers by department later. It's okay, we won't judge. Second, determine how much money, on average, each customer spent at the dealership. Third, how long, on average, have they been your customer? For most dealerships, this is about ten years, but you can determine a more accurate number for your dealership by picking a handful of customers and looking at how long they have been active customers at your dealership and then averaging the number.

The total number of customers is typically the number of specific family units that buy from you. Again, if your people are CRM ninjas, this will be an easy number for you to grab. If not, start by tracking these numbers over the next week and utilize that information to give you a place to start from.

Second, divide the number of total customers in the one-year period by the gross revenue for that same year. This gives you a rough idea of what each customer (or family unit) spends with you every year.

Then, multiply that number by the average time the customer stays your customer.

So, here is how this breaks down.

Let's say you have had two thousand customers (or families) buy from the dealership over the past year, and you have generated gross revenue of $1 million during that same time. You know that the average customer stays with your dealership for ten years. (I know this may be bringing back terrible memories of math word problems, but stick with me, I promise you won't have to figure out any train speeds in this one.)

$1 million gross revenue / 2,000 customers = $500 per customer

$500 per customer x 10 years = $5,000 Customer Lifetime Value

Once you know the average dollar amount a customer will generate for you during the time they remain your customer, you are able to make better, well-informed decisions as to how much marketing you should spend to acquire them in the first place.

Let's look at it this way. If you know that it costs $300 to acquire a new customer and that the customer will spend approximately $1,000 a year and remain your customer for ten years, the customer lifetime value of a single customer is $10,000. Then, ask yourself, is $300 a good investment to acquire the new customer? Yes! When you are able to see and understand the numbers, it allows you to make the best-informed decisions for your dealership.

TAKE YOUR PROFIT FIRST

Many of the dealers we work with put themselves last. They put everything and everyone else first—their employees, their expenses, their sanity—until there is nothing left at the end of the month for them. When we start talking about cash flow, it's not uncommon to hear an audible gasp, as this is a subject that dealers don't want to touch with a ten-foot pole. In my mind, I think that's because there are major misconceptions around cash flow and money in a dealership. Many times, it starts with your employees. Your employees assume that, since you own the dealership, you go home at the end of the night and count your piles of cash, which is all locked in a secret room in your house that you designed specifically for that purpose. If you are doing that, more power to you; but, if you're not, you are like most dealers around the country.

While your employees might see money coming into the dealership, what most employees don't see is the large amounts of money going out of the dealership. They assume that since you sell X number of units a year, you just put that money directly into your pocket. They don't see the cost of the equipment, payroll, payroll taxes, liability insurance, workers compensation, building maintenance, or any of the other hundreds of expenses you have to pay from your ever-thinning margins. They may assume you are filthy rich with no care in the world and can't reconcile why you aren't driving an expensive sports car to the dealership every single day. We all know that the scenario many of your employees have created in their heads may not be reality.

The struggle, many times, is how you bridge this gap of the misconceptions that the people around you (and maybe even you) have around money management inside of your dealership, with the changes that need to happen in order to have a profitable and thriving business. And heck, a happy and full bank account.

So, let's work on changing the misconceptions that you walk into your dealership with, and start taking your profit before anything else. The idea of taking your profit first may seem a little (or a lot) overwhelming. So, how do you do this without feeling like you are going to faint every time?

1. Make the decision that things aren't going to remain the same.

In Habit One, we talked about our surviving-versus-thriving vision. Surviving is a fine place to be, but not a place you want to stay. You are not doing anyone any favors being the last one paid, or not being paid at all. You have put too much work into your dealership for it not to provide you with the life you want. So, plan to take your profit first. Step one is to make the all-in, scary decision that you are going to make a change. This means that you choose, from now on, to pay yourself first, even when things seem like they are getting tight.

What you are getting ready to do makes a lot of logical sense from a numbers standpoint, but emotionally it will feel uncomfortable. As you begin this process and experience this discomfort, you will have to make the decision over and over again that you are going to require your business to pay you before anything else gets paid. So long are the years of looking at your P & L statement and seeing that you made a profit but have no idea where it went. So long to paying yourself but not cashing the checks. You are going to know exactly where it went because you are taking it out on a regular basis.

The decision you are getting ready to make is that you, maybe for the very first time, are going to take control of your cash flow, and not let your cash flow take control of you. How do you do this? You do this by creating a budget that pays you first. What is left, after you are paid, is what you have available to pay your employees and the other expenses that come with running your dealership. What do you do if there isn't enough? You need to either increase your revenue or decrease your expenses. I wish there was more to it, but there isn't. You have to make the decision to deal with being uncomfortable, so that you can gain control of your sanity, your life, and your dealership.

Do you know what the easier, but disastrous, option is? Letting your cash flow take control of you. Do you know what will help you be profitable and help you sleep better at night? You, taking control of your cash flow. It's up to you. Do you want easy or do you want money in the bank? This decision is solely up to you.

2. Start with 1 percent.

So, you decided to choose money in the bank, over easy, or at least you are really starting to consider it. How do we start? How is it that after this decision your bank account will start reflecting the choice?

To start, I want you to pick a percentage that you, as an owner, are going to take as profit or retained earnings out of your business, as well as a salary. It doesn't need to be big, but I need you to get used to taking a paycheck. So often, the dealership owners we work with take a little here and there out of the business, wait until the end of the year, and hope to see something left in the bank account.

So, instead of taking the approach that doesn't work, pick a percentage that you want to set aside as profit or retained earnings, and an amount of salary that you deserve for all of your personal investment, risk, and liability. Then, off the top of your budget, deduct the percentage you've decided on from the profit that is produced and set it aside. Then, deduct the amount of your pay. The portion that's left is what you are going to operate your business on.

If just simply reading this is giving you incredible anxiety and possibly heart palpitations, start with 1 percent off the top. That's it. One percent of every dollar of profit produced in your dealership should be deposited in a separate bank account. This money is for your use. You can hold it as retained earnings, pay yourself as a distribution or dividend, or maybe begin to reimburse yourself for money you have previously invested into the dealership. How you do this may be decided by how your business is set up: sole proprietorship, LLC, S Corp, or C Corp. Connect with your CPA to make sure you are taking this money out of the business in the correct way for your situation.

Here's an example of what this looks like. Let's say you expect to gross $100,000 in revenue next month. From that you generated $9,000 of gross profit in sales, $10,000 in parts gross profit, and $7,500 in service gross profit. You now have a $26,500 pool of gross profit to run your dealership for the month. You would take 1 percent out of that amount ($265). Then, let's say you plan to pay yourself $3,000. You would deduct that amount.

$26,500 − $265 − $3,000 = $23,235

This leaves you $23,235 to operate the dealership on for the month.

Moving forward, look at the next month. You know the season will begin to slow down and you anticipate bringing in only $80,000. Using the same percentages as before, sales would produce $7,200 of gross profit, parts would produce $9,600 in gross profit, and service would produce $6,000 in gross profit.

So, your gross profit pool now has $22,800 in it. Take the 1 percent ($228) and set it aside. Deduct your gross salary of $3,000 and the rest ($19,572) is what you have to run your dealership on for the month ($22,800 − $228 − $3,000 = $19,572).

If you fear it will not be enough, then now is the time to consider how to increase revenue or decrease expenses. No matter what, don't leave yourself out of the equation. This will force you to consider other approaches to fix the problem. If you are wondering how I came up with the gross profit numbers, I used our balanced dealership approach. As we work with dealers, we work to have 60 percent of gross revenue generated by sales, 25 percent by parts, and 15 percent through service. I used a 15 percent gross profit margin on sales, a 40 percent gross profit on parts, and a 50 percent gross profit on labor. We will talk about this more in depth in the next habit.

The most important part of the exercise is that you created a habit of paying yourself first. Is 1 percent where it ends? Absolutely not. You should work toward the goal of putting 10 percent of every profit dollar produced into your pocket. I know that seems like a huge number when you are simply celebrating a 1 percent payment to yourself, but it is possible.

Something interesting starts to happen when you give the business less money to run on. You and your team will find a way to adjust expenses and force your business to run on what is available (or you will find new ways to make money).

Think about it this way. If you were given a brand-new tube of toothpaste, how would you use it? At first, you might be overly generous with the amount of toothpaste you put on your toothbrush. If some extra fell off and landed in the sink, it wouldn't be a big deal. However, if I were to give you a tube of toothpaste with only a small amount of toothpaste left in it and you couldn't go buy any more for at least a week, how long could you make it last? My guess is as long as you needed. In fact, I bet you could make that toothpaste last two more weeks! When you feel like there is an excess of resources available to you, you typically get careless in using them. However, when you feel like what you have is scarce, you use it more wisely. That's exactly the mindset shift that I need you to take on in regard to your money. Take what you should off the top and learn to run the dealership on what is then available or left over.

3. Put your 1 percent (or more) somewhere you won't touch it, and have someone hold you accountable.

Where you put your money is equally as important as taking the money out. Now, I'm not saying an account in the Bahamas is the answer; that just looks shady. But you can't leave your money in the same account that you pay your expenses out of (or an account where you will be tempted to loan it right back to the dealership—we know you do this!) because you know as well as I do that the money will be simply absorbed, and your hard work and determination will be all for nothing. When that happens, you feel defeated and wonder why you even tried.

So, open a separate account simply for this money. That's all you want to put into this account. Maybe you know yourself well enough to know that a separate account at the same bank won't do and you need to move the money to a different bank that is not linked in any way to the business. If that's what you need to do, just do it. There is no judgment here. Our focus is simply that we want you to get in the rhythm of having your business pay you, as the owner, on every single profit dollar that is generated each month.

Some of the dealers we work with go one step further when starting to implement this change. One of our advisors has his dealers send him a picture of the "off the top" check as proof that they are taking it out of the business. Above that, he asks them to tell him what they are going to use the money for. Sometimes it is to accomplish a goal they have set, maybe it is designated for something fun, or at other times it's simply to help them survive. Now, you may or may not need that accountability, but I will tell you, if you aren't currently paying yourself on a regular basis from your business, at first, it will feel strange. And, if you need someone to tell you that it's okay to pay yourself first, I'm here to tell you, IT'S OKAY!! In fact, it's critical.

4. Consider doing something fun with the money you are earning (at least in a small way).

The last step is the best step. This is where you get to dream a little. Think about something you would like to do and how you could use this money on something you and your family would enjoy. Maybe it can go toward a vacation or furniture fund, savings for a lake house, or just a night out at your favorite restaurant. You have worked hard to generate this revenue in your business, and now is your time to celebrate your hard work, risk, and focus. So, pick something fun and do it.

Now we need to turn our attention to another matter. Let's say that after you take out your salary, there is not enough money to cover all your expenses, specifically your employee expense. It might be that you are overpaying your people. Let's walk through how you should calculate what each employee, by department, should be earning.

UTILIZE SALARY CAPS
FOR EVERY DEPARTMENT

Each role, in each department, has a different salary cap, or amount, that you can afford to pay based upon the income of that department. Think about your dealership like a professional sports team. You, as the GM, only have a certain amount of money available to pay for your players (or employees). When you reach the cap, you simply cannot pay any more. So how do you determine salary caps? Well, salary caps vary by department and role, but when you understand where the numbers come from, it allows you to set the pay of your employees up in a way that allows them to make a great living, while allowing you to make a substantial profit. When you step over the cap, your profits begin to disappear rapidly.

Let's start by taking a look at your service department.

You can determine your salary caps for your technicians by looking at your posted labor rate.

Your posted labor rate breaks down like this:

Thirty percent of your posted labor rate goes to paying the technician. So, if you have a $100/hour posted labor rate, the maximum pay, or salary cap, for your technician is $30/hour (this includes base pay plus bonuses), if they are 100 percent efficient. We talked about how to calculate that earlier in the chapter.

What happens if you need to pay a technician more than what you have allotted? You need to move your labor rate up. That's it. Because your salary cap is 30 percent of your posted labor rate, we can't go above the salary cap or we start eating into the profits that we have set aside.

Fifteen percent of every single labor dollar produced goes toward your management cost in your service department. If you have a service manager, this is where you will be able to figure out your salary cap for them. As a note, in order to cost-justify a service manager you need a minimum of three technicians who are at least 85 percent efficient. If you aren't there, you would have a service writer who the 15 percent would be set aside for.

Again, if you have three technicians and your posted labor rate is $100/hour, that means you can take $15/hour per technician to pay your service manager, service writer, and service coordinator, giving you a salary cap of $45/hour.

Thirty-five percent of every labor dollar produced should go toward departmental costs such as insurance, payroll taxes, utilities, rent, and other overhead required to keep our service department functioning. This means if your labor rate is $100/hour you would set aside $35/hour billed to take care of these expenses. This should be set aside, in a separate account, and only used for these items.

Twenty percent of the net profit should be set aside for the owner. We talked about the importance of taking profit earlier, but this is incredibly important. So, if your labor rate is $100/hour we would expect you to take $20/hour produced in your shop. This means if you have three technicians who produce eight hours of work from your service department a day you should be taking $480 a day as net profit from your service department.

Here is what this would look like with three technicians at 100 percent efficiency and a $100/hour labor rate.

$2,400—Service Revenue for the Day

$720—Technician Pay (30 percent)

$840—Departmental Costing (35 percent)

$360—Management Cost (15 percent)

$480—Owner Profit (20 percent)

Once you understand the basics of the salary caps, determining what you can pay employees in the parts and sales departments becomes simple. In both departments the salary caps are based upon a percentage of gross profit. Depending upon your gross profit margin, your parts salary cap can run from 25 percent to 30 percent of total gross profit. That is what you have available for the labor cost of running that department. If you are a new dealer with few parts sales, the person at the parts counter is more than likely helping in service writing and maybe even selling. You will need to offset their cost by using the salary caps from the other two departments.

Just as in parts, your sales salary cap is a function of a percentage of your gross profit. Again, because your margins will vary by industry your salary cap will run from a low of 20 percent to a high of 25 percent of the gross profit produced. Regardless of parts or sales, your goal is to work to drive 10 percent of the gross profit back to the owner as profit after departmental expenses.

WHAT DOES THIS LOOK LIKE?

Once you understand the numbers coming out of your dealership, you have to find a way to empower your people to understand the numbers as well. We are going to talk about transparency with your people in the last habit, but I want you to start thinking about what you need to do to become the teacher you needed for yourself on this topic. Maybe what you will need to move forward is simply pulling the right reports from your management software, finding someone to walk alongside you, or just becoming consistent in pulling the numbers. Regardless, you need to become fluent in these numbers.

Like you, your people probably didn't join your team because they were excited to dive into numbers. Your people may have varying degrees of understanding regarding the numbers and terminology. They may have come from a previous dealership where the conversations around numbers and budgets were always negative or harsh. Take a step back and understand what knowledge and experience your people have regarding numbers. Remember, one of your primary responsibilities is to develop your people. That involves teaching them to think like you do and communicating effectively. The only way you can achieve that is with time and intentionality. When you do, you will take control of your business, as Ron and Kyle did. Now when we talk with them, they can recite their numbers on the spot. They are finally able to focus on other areas of their dealership and enjoy the life they have worked hard to create. Are you ready to join them?

HABIT FIVE:

Maintain a Positive Attitude and Take Action

I'M THE PROBLEM: *Why even bother?*
I'M THE SOLUTION: *We're a mean, lean cash-generating machine.*

I have known Michael for over fifteen years. He worked in the corporate world, while his father and grandfather ran a family-owned dealership. His father was persistent in asking Michael to join them. Eventually he made the decision to leave his career and do just that. When Michael and I first met, I was speaking at a distributors meeting that he was attending in Tennessee.

At lunch I was looking for an open spot when I saw Michael waving for me to sit at his table with him and a few other dealers. During lunch, I learned a lot about Michael, his attitude, and his passion for his dealership. Before working at the dealership, Michael had worked with a large fast-food chain as a regional manager. His job was to work with new franchises and help them with all aspects of getting their business off the ground. From employees, to marketing, to dealing with their competition, Michael was the go-to guy.

Since joining the dealership, he had been struggling to help them move the business to that next level. He said, "Bob, I don't feel like much of what I have done in my previous career applies to what I need to do now for the dealership." I told him that everything he has done applies; he just has to think about the dealership like it was a fast-food restaurant.

"Think of your food prep area like your shop," I told him. "How important were processes in the food prep area to make a store effective in both your drive-through and customer counter?"

Michael said, "It was critical for both the quality of the food and the ability to quickly get good food out."

"How about in your drive-through—what were the two most important things to your customers?"

He said, "Getting the right food that was ordered and doing it fast."

And finally, I asked, "What was your goal for customers who chose to dine in and order at the counter?"

"Well, we wanted them to not feel rushed, so they could take time, enjoy their food and the atmosphere of the store we worked to create."

"Bingo!" I said. "Just do the same thing you have been doing for years and you will grow to not only the next level but will end up adding additional locations. He laughed at the idea of another location, but I could tell his mind was already rethinking ways he could grow the dealership.

Through the years, Michael and I have become good friends. His dealership was just outside of a major metropolitan city and is now a dynamic force in the area. I don't want you to think that Michael had an easy journey, because it hasn't been. He had to deal with an employee theft issue that cost them nearly $100,000. A large competitor, who was located in the city and a good distance from him, decided to expand into Michael's territory. They gave him a choice to either sell out to them, at a ridiculous price, or just be run out of business. Michael laughed at them.

The challenge created by the competitor brought out the creative side of Michael. During the next two years his competitor tried to drive him out of business by selling equipment at cost. He worked hard at creating loyalty with his customers by innovating with new programs that rewarded customers who purchased from him. It was not long before customers he had lost began returning to his dealership. They desired great customer service and a shop they could count on to fix their equipment. As they returned, he welcomed each customer back, like a prodigal son, and took care of the issues on the equipment even if it had been purchased from the competitor.

Over the course of time, Michael had taken on a partner and had grown the dealership from one store, to a second store, and then a third store. The third store had been open just a few months, when Michael got a call. One of their drivers had been in an accident. He was texting while driving and had rear-ended a car, killing one of the passengers and seriously injuring a second. Of all the tests that life had brought him over the years I had known him, this one was the toughest.

I hadn't spoken to Michael for several months when I got his call. He caught me up on all that had happened. After the accident, he learned that their liability insurance only provided $2 million in coverage. He and his partner were being sued for $10 million.

While Michael and his partner had their three stores separated legally, the original store, the store that was started by his dad and granddad, was the one being sued and the one that was the most profitable. From start to finish it was a two-year ordeal that he battled through. As I talked with him over those two years, I was always amazed at his attitude. He battled through some very dark days, and yet, at the end of each of our phone calls, his positive attitude become an inspiration to me.

Michael had applied all he had learned from his corporate life into the running of the dealerships. He had grown his people to be able to run the stores without him or his partner, as they directed all their focus on trying to keep the dealerships alive. His processes were in place; he had a great banker and great manufacturers who continued to support him by giving him time and flexibility to deal with floorplan issues and lines of credit because of the lawsuit.

I believe it was Michael's never-give-up attitude, his ability to separate his emotion from the day-to-day challenges he faced, his willingness to lean on outside people for advice and counsel, his ability to come up with creative solutions to new problems, and his faith that, after two long years, brought everything to a conclusion.

Does the story have a perfect ending? Unfortunately, no. A life was lost, a person severely injured, and a young man was sentenced to prison, all because of a moment in time when a driver was distracted by a text. Michael had to close his newest store and focus all his energy on the one store, his father's store, that was at risk. When he was back working on reviving this store, Michael found a trusted employee who was stealing from him and that he had to terminate.

The stress on Michael, his family, and his team was enormous, and yet he continued to maintain a positive attitude and approached the future with confidence. Currently, Michael and his partner are working on reopening the third store and to continue the original plan of dominating their marketplace. As for me, there is no doubt in my mind that he will make it happen.

• • •

What Bob is saying is true. Dealers who are profitable have an objective and positive view of all that is going on in their dealership, and they are able to make decisions without letting emotion lead them astray. Letting emotions guide your decisions is the easy thing to do. Think about it. How many times have you made a bad decision because you relied on your emotions instead of logic? Probably a lot.

As a quick example, I want you to think about the following situations and how you would respond to them.

1. A customer walks in and says your dealership should be on an episode of *Hoarders*.
2. An employee who is always on your nerves screws up with one of your biggest customers.
3. The competitive dealer puts up an obnoxious billboard right across the road from your store.
4. The big box stores sell a product or a part for less than you can buy it.

The response to each of these things typically will get an emotional reaction instead of a logical one. Also, each of these things has happened to dealerships we work with. The thing that separates dealers who can deal with the torrent of frustrating situations that come through their doors each day from those who get swept into the whirlwind of frustration and a knee-jerk reaction is that they take an objective look at what's going on and they don't let their emotions overtake the situation.

YOU CAN'T OUT-LOGIC EMOTION

Time and time again we see dealers making decisions based upon emotion instead of using logic. From keeping a toxic employee because they have become a part of the family, to letting a son verbally abuse employees to the point that all of their good people left and they were stuck with employees who were willing to take the abuse so they could just get a paycheck. Emotionally it was the easy way out—just leave things as they are and hope it changes, instead of using logic to conclude, "This isn't going to improve, and I need to take action to change the direction I am currently heading."

Years ago, I heard the phrase "You can't out-logic emotion." I don't know where I was or who said it, but the phrase has stuck with me. I have come to realize that most people, as they have grown up and matured, have been taught the skill of de-escalating their personal emotions when encountering an emotional situation. This allows them to make logical decisions and have a reasonable reaction. I know it might seem like some of your customers or employees haven't learned this yet, but my guess is, they probably just haven't had to practice it much.

I don't know what your go-to way is to de-escalate your emotions in a situation, but I know everyone has different strategies. For you, maybe it involves sitting down and creating a pros-and-cons list, or taking an evening jog. Perhaps you distance yourself from the situation through a favorite show or watching sports. Or maybe it's talking to someone who isn't close to the situation so is able to provide objectivity.

As you go through this chapter, I need you to trust me.

Keep your emotions in check and allow me to be the logic or sounding board for you as we talk about the things in this chapter. I want—no, need—you to trust me as we walk through this chapter. As we start talking about things like your people, products, and services, I have a pretty good guess of what's going to happen. If you are like most dealers, you are going to start getting defensive and your emotions are going to take control.

Now, hear me out. This isn't a bad thing, because it means you care, but my guess is you'll think or say or shout, "Not me! That's not how my dealership works." And, maybe you're right. But what I do know is one of the superpowers of those who run a profitable dealership is that of maintaining an objective view of their dealership. A view that allows you to see the forest among the trees, and I want to be your guide. So, let's take a look at your dealership objectively.

SAFEGUARDING YOUR DEALERSHIP

When you begin to objectively look at your business, one area that is often overlooked is that of safeguarding your dealership. Now, I get it. No one likes a Debby Downer, or someone who always feels like the other shoe is going to drop, but we also need to be realistic and realize that things don't always go according to plan.

We are writing this book in the middle of the COVID-19 pandemic, when much of the world is having to work out of their homes. Through this, you and I have learned firsthand about the uncertainty of the future; we never see events coming but when they arrive, they alter the way we do business from that moment forward. As an owner or manager, you have the responsibility to your family, your people, and your community to be adequately prepared for these disrupting events.

Strive for Balance in Your Dealership

One way to safeguard your dealership is to focus on creating balance; this means that every department is responsible for generating enough income so that, regardless of what may happen, at least two of your three departments can keep you afloat. Now, achieving this balance isn't easy. But normally the things that bring you the most peace of mind in your business aren't easy. When we start working with a dealership, we begin by looking at their balance, or lack thereof, because this tells us where the dealership is strong, but also where the vulnerabilities or weaknesses lie.

In some industries, there is a lot of talk around the concept of absorption in the dealership, meaning that the parts and service, or the aftermarket departments, can sustain all the dealership's expenses. While in an ideal world we would love to see that, we also understand that not all the dealerships have consistent revenue all year long and thus our focus is balance instead of absorption. So, if one of the departments is slower, the other two still are able to sustain the dealership.

Let's break down what we typically look for when we talk about balance in a dealership. You can find out where your dealership stacks up by pulling your year-end numbers by department and figuring what percentage of total revenue each department represents. I know, "Sara, you are back into the numbers again!" Just trust me on this. Go ahead and roll your eyes, but I still need you to pull out your end-of-the-year profit-and-loss (income) statement, so we can do some math.

SALES/WHOLE GOODS – TARGET: 60 PERCENT OF REVENUE

Let's start with the sales department. Whenever we start walking through this process with a dealership, we typically see that they have 80 percent of their revenue being generated from whole goods. Now, depending on what lines you carry, margins will vary, but most of our dealers are making margins of anywhere from 8 percent to 18 percent on the units they are selling. I know that is a big swing, but we work in a lot of different industries. Our focus is to get our sales department to represent 60 percent of all revenue being generated by the dealership as a whole.

Does this mean we should sell less all for the sake of balance? Absolutely not. We move this percentage down by increasing the amount and margins of the parts we are selling, and the profitability of the service work we do.

PARTS—TARGET: 25 PERCENT OF REVENUE

In the parts department, our goal is to have 25 percent of our total revenue generated from parts sales both online and in-store. Depending on your industry, we see anywhere from a 35 percent to 55+ percent margin on parts. When we start working with dealers on creating balance, it's not uncommon to see only 15 percent of revenue coming out of the parts department, due to margins not being tight and a lack of focus on upselling and cross selling. However, we know that one of the indicators of a healthy dealership is that the parts department not only generates 25 percent of the total revenue for the dealership but has strong margins.

SERVICE—TARGET: 15 PERCENT OF REVENUE

The service department should generate 15 percent of the gross revenue for the dealership. Our goal is that all service work has a minimum of a 50 percent margin. That's huge. That can only be accomplished by focusing on the numbers we talked about in the previous chapter and implementing processes to help your technicians be efficient. Some strategies to increase your efficiencies may be pricing your work by the job instead of by the hour, flat rating, and making sure you don't have your best technician on time and material work, without multiplying it by his or her average efficiency when doing flat-rate work. When we start working with a dealer, it's not uncommon for us to see only 5 percent of the revenue, for the dealership as a whole, coming from the service department.

So, how balanced is your dealership? Pull out your numbers from last year and see what percentage of the total money produced came from each department.

What area needs to be your focus to help push you toward balance? Again, balance in your dealership won't be created overnight, but what will happen is that over time your dealership will be able to withstand a weather event, an economic downturn, or just about anything that might come at you once you achieve departmental balance.

Evaluate Your Insurance

While I don't know of many owners who are excited about paying for insurance, in our years of experience in working with dealerships, insurance is one area that most owners fail to evaluate properly each year. A change in location, a change in ownership, or if there is an increased or decreased ability to deal with risk—all of those are compelling reasons to look over your policy.

Let's revisit Michael's situation with his insurance coverage. Years ago, when Michael had one store, $2 million of liability coverage seemed like a lot. Three stores and fifteen years later it wasn't even close to the amount he needed when he was faced with a $10 million lawsuit. While we would tell you that you should always be watchful of your expenses, in all our years in working with dealers we have never had one dealer who filed a claim and said, "I can't believe I was covered so well!" While it might be tempting to evaluate insurance based upon simply the cost of the policy, it's just as important to make sure that you have the right coverage and not just a policy that is the right price.

We had two different dealerships this year that unfortunately had major claims on their insurance policies. One had the right coverage; the other did not. The difference in how the two policies impacted their dealerships were stark. A dealership we work with in New Hampshire had a catastrophic fire that burned their dealership to the ground. The dad and his son, a marine veteran, had the right insurance and the right connections in their state. (They both are great at building relationship in their community.) And in short order they had the old structure removed, set up a mobile trailer for their office, and were working with their insurance company, their manufacturers, and their local, county, and state governments. After all was said and done, they were able to come back bigger and stronger than ever.

Compare that to a dealership that didn't have the right coverage. This was a fast-growing dealership that was sitting on a floodplain. Their agent had failed to mention they should consider flood insurance (he wanted to keep their costs low); and just this spring, the floods came and destroyed hundreds of thousands of dollars in customer units as well as new units. All of their technicians' tools were covered with water and silt, and none had any insurance on their own tools. Just as this dealership was in a position to explode and grow, mother nature had a different plan. The impact on the dealership and the couple running it was devastating. While the flood would have still happened, with the right coverage, they would have been made whole. Now they are back to square one.

So, where do you start? Get a copy of your insurance policies and read them instead of depending on your insurance agent to tell you what is in them. I know this doesn't sound like a good time, but the headache and dollars you save will be worth the momentary inconvenience. This is part of your strategy on how you are going to achieve your vision. Make sure that as you go through them the dealership name is correct, the address is correct, and the coverage is listed accurately and what you expected it to be. If there is anything wrong with the name, location, or coverage, and you need to file a claim, the insurance company is going to use the policy, not what the agent told you, as the basis for how they will settle your claim.

Evaluate the deductible. Most owners choose a high deductible to reduce the cost of the policy. If you are a struggling new dealer with tight cash flow, you might be better off with a higher payment and a lower deductible. While the premium will be higher, it will reduce the potential out-of-pocket expenses that you may not be able to afford if the claim happens during your slow, low cash flow part of the season. If you are an established dealer with good cash flow and reserves, then taking on more of the risk with a high deductible might make sense. There is not a one-size-fits-all solution when it comes to your insurance deductible. Make sure your deductible is an amount that you could afford if you had to file a claim at the peak of your slow season.

While insurance may not be an exciting part of running your dealership, having the correct insurance to minimize your risk will help you sleep at night and ensure that, if you do have to file a claim in the future, your dealership and employees will be able to continue producing revenue.

Re-evaluate the Value of Your Customers

If you could run your dealership and not have to deal with customers, would you? The answer for most of you is probably yes. No, I can't read your mind, even though it might seem like it.

When you started your dealership, your customers were very important to you. You treated them like kings and queens and greeted them with great fanfare (and maybe tea and crumpets, which are similar to English muffins for my American readers). But you may have noticed that the longer you have been in business, the more of a nuisance they have become, and you only put up with them because you want their money.

It may be time to set your sights back on your customers and fully grasp that your business couldn't exist without them. As painful as it might seem, when you are dealing with a difficult customer, you need them. Once you deal with these hard realities in therapy, you need to make sure you and your people have a change in attitude and begin to truly value your customers again. And through your actions, your customer will experience this positive change in attitude as well.

One way to help customers understand how much you value them is by creating a loyalty program.

Think about how many stores have a "shopper card" or a "preferred customer" program. These stores are marking up prices on some items to be able to give discounts on other items. We all understand that, but it still makes the customers feel like they are getting a perk for doing business at the store.

I want to challenge you to think about creating a similar program for your dealership. While a customer loyalty program may not be right for every dealer, it is a program that we have found many customers will get excited about and actively participate in. So, what does a customer loyalty program include?

First, have plastic cards printed with your logo on them and have "preferred customer" somewhere across the middle. These cards can be purchased inexpensively, online. With the right vendor, designing them can be easy. Once you have them in hand, you will give them to customers who purchase a unit from you, which, for most dealerships, will automatically enroll them into the loyalty program. Most people today don't want to fill out any more forms than necessary, so let them opt in, and take care of the details for them.

Then, decide on the benefits of your program. A few things to include in your customer loyalty program are:

1. *A discounted labor rate:* Set your labor rate for non-purchasing customers. A non-purchasing customer is anyone who bought at another dealership, but they still want you to do the service on the equipment. Then, discount a percentage off the labor rate for customers that purchased from you. As an example, if your posted labor rate is currently $100/hour, move it to $110 for non-purchasing customers and then, through your preferred customer program, give purchasing customers a $10/hour discount.

2. *Priority in the service department:* Give the customers who purchase from you priority in the service department. If someone brings a product in for service or repair, and they didn't buy from you, they will go behind a customer who bought from you even if the non-purchasing customer was next in line.

3. *Discounted parts:* Consider offering a discount on parts that are installed in the service department. In our Preferred Customer Programs the customer receives a 5 percent discount on all parts installed. Later I will share the importance of adding an extra 5 percent on the parts you sell to your own service department and explain why the extra percentage is important to offsetting the extra time it takes to sell a part to yourself versus selling it to a costumer across your parts counter.

4. *Volume bonus:* You may also want to create a volume bonus program for your municipalities or commercial customers. With your customer loyalty program, they can earn additional discounts on parts based upon their volume of purchases as the year progresses. One thing that many of our dealers do is pool the customers' bonus for the entire year and, near the end of the year, send the individual/ organization a check with their bonuses. This is a great way to stay top of mind during the holidays. When everyone else is sending out lame calendars (please, don't send out calendars!), you are sending out rebate checks to your top customers. It will be the exact same amount they would have received month by month, but now it's one nice check. Trust me, they will love it.

It's important to train your team to recognize the Preferred Customer Program or loyalty cards and be able to answer questions regarding the benefits of joining the program. When starting a new program, customers will want information before enrolling, and they are going to want to know what the process will be like. Your focus should be to have your team well-trained on the program and to keep enrollment easy.

Keep a log of who has enrolled. This can be done through a drop-down menu in your Dealer Management Software or simply an Excel document on your computer.

Keep in mind, this program can also be a great selling tool. When working with salespeople, one of the things we say over and over is that you shouldn't negotiate with cash, when at all possible. We are crazy about this because when you negotiate with cash, you have a 100 percent margin you are losing. So, you need different negotiation strategies. If you have a customer, and service is important to them, you can use this program to help them see how it's worth the additional money they would pay upfront for the priority and discount on service they will receive in the long run.

You are able to give these customers discounts because they gave you the opportunity to pick up some of the margins on the front end of the sale, and the customers who decided to buy elsewhere simply won't have the same perks.

We typically only recommend that you extend the benefits of this program to pre-selected products that the customer purchased directly from you. I understand that some dealers want all of their customers, whether they purchased or not, to have the same experience. Just to be clear, we want all customers who come into your store to have a "wow" experience. But we believe those customers who paid more to buy from you should have some perks—that's all we are trying to do with the Preferred Customer Program.

An effortless way to make customers aware of your program is by putting up a sign in the sales area that says, "Ask about the benefits of being a preferred customer!" This simple type of marketing generates revenue because customers are willing to spend more on products because of the perks they will receive in the future.

Implementing a Preferred Customer Program for your customers is a simple way to remind them that they are a valued part of the dealership, and without them, you wouldn't be able to offer your services to the community. The little extras your Preferred Customers get is a nice reminder for both you and them that the spark that started when they purchased from you in the beginning is still glowing even after the sale is done.

Employees

Placing value on your employees is critically important, but I know that's probably not a shock to you. You would not be able to serve your customers without them, and what your employees bring to the dealership is what differentiates you from the next dealer. One thing I know to be true is that you, as an owner or manager, care deeply about your people and their well-being. In most cases, your employees have become like family to you. One of the tricky things about family is, sometimes we don't give them the credit they deserve. Often, they take the brunt of the complaints and criticism. Other times, they knock it out of the park but rarely get the credit they deserve.

You must change your mindset and begin to value your employees and show them that they are important to you and the dealership. When you have this conscious (because it won't happen if you're not thinking about it) and consistent (because initially they will think you just read a book and are implementing new things that will never stick) shift, they will begin to realize that you do value them, and that you also want them to be proud of what they contribute to the dealership and the community.

While I'm not sure what situation you are in with your employees, I do know there is hope. Maybe you have the best team you have ever had and are proud of the work they do. That's great.

Keep raising the bar. But maybe that's not your situation. Maybe you feel like your people continue to walk all over you and hold you hostage, leaving you as the one who has to put out all the fires. In our world, if this is the case, there are only two options. You've heard us say this before and it is worth mentioning again: you either change the people or change the people.

When you make the conscious decision that you are going to be part of the solution, and adjust your attitude about your dealership, your customers, and your employees, and truly value all that you have, you will be met with a flurry of events that will test your resolve. The greatest challenge will be with people (both customers and your employees) who refuse to understand this shift or to get on board. Ultimately, you are the only person who can be in control of how you respond to this, but if you want to be the solution rather than the problem, it's up to you to make sure your attitude and action match what you are saying.

Most of the dealerships we work with sell a high-quality product, provide excellent service, and have stocked the right parts for customers, and they charge a premium price for those services. The struggle that many dealerships run into is keeping the professionalism of your team at the level it needs to be to justify a premium price.

How Your People Look =
How Customers Perceive the Value of Your Dealership

Answer this for me: If you were a customer walking into your dealership today, how much money would you feel comfortable giving your employees?

Your presentation and the personal presentation of your people is important in how customers perceive your business. That may sound like an obvious statement, but the core of it is this: if you want your dealership to be a business that gets a premium price for your whole goods, parts, and service, you and your people have to look the part. That means the person behind the parts counter with the "Satan rules" T-shirt needs to go put on a dealership polo and be happy about it. People get nervous spending thousands of dollars with someone who looks like they have never seen that amount of money in their life. This is something called incongruency.

Have you ever had an experience where you are logically ready to move forward with a decision, but something that you couldn't put your finger on made you hesitate? No, I'm not talking about your wedding. Maybe you have seen this play out in your dealership. A customer walks in to buy a product. The salesperson starts talking and says you are going to love this product. It's going to do all of the things you need it to do. The salesperson is saying the right thing, "You are going to love this product," but his head is subtly shaking back and forth in a "no" motion. The customer says to themselves, "Hmm. I do think this is the right product, but something doesn't seem right about the situation." They decide to wait, or worse, they ask for a brochure. This is a congruency issue. Also, if you are reading this saying, "My salespeople would never do that!" go watch them and then sign them up for sales training!

The dealership, the look of your people, the ways they interact and present themselves must all be congruent. Then, customers will feel more comfortable spending their money with you.

Personal presentation goes far beyond physical appearance, even though that is a major component. The professionalism of your people when they interact with customers on the phone or through email is also incredibly important. Do you have standards that you require your people to abide by?

Not long ago I called a dealership that we have worked with for years. An employee answered the phone both abruptly and sharply with "ABC Dealership" (names have been changed to protect the innocent). My first thought? Whose funeral did I interrupt? Because his tone, at that moment, made me think I was the biggest inconvenience that had ever happened in his life. Because I know the people at this dealership, I knew that wasn't the case. But, it is a good reminder to look at all the ways you communicate with customers and ask if your people's presentation in each department is actually exhibiting who you are as a dealership.

Ask yourself these questions:

- If I were to walk into my dealership as a customer, would I be comfortable giving any of my employees' $1,000, $10,000, $100,000? Where is the breaking point and why?
- What is being portrayed by my employees when they answer the phone?
- What standards do I have for my employees, and are they aware of them?
- Am I utilizing my employee handbook?

You may be thinking, "Well, I know this is true, but how do I implement this change?"

First, set your expectations. What do you expect from your employees in regard to dress, personal appearance, and communication? Do you even know? Once you decide, communicate that to them. Communicate consistently and point out people who have done a good job of portraying the image you want your dealership to have. There is something powerful about positive reinforcement. It takes you very little time to tell someone they are doing a good job, it costs you nothing, and it yields great results. Regardless who you are, you can fit that into the budget.

The next thing you need to do is make sure your expectations are clearly outlined in your employee handbook. I know, an employee handbook sounds like a lot of work and not a lot of fun. But you have to keep in mind that your employee handbook is the process for your HR department. I am aware that many dealerships don't have employee handbooks. I get it. You didn't start your dealership because you loved dealing with HR issues and paperwork. However, the HR side of the business is going to be there as long as you aren't your only employee. On the flip side, anything you don't address means you allow, and you will be forced to deal with it later, I guarantee it. An employee handbook will go a long way in alleviating many future headaches, without the use of Tylenol.

If an employee comes to you and has a question about really anything, it's a glaring warning sign, similar to a bank alarm or a tornado siren going off. It tells you there is a breakdown in process. The fact that the employee didn't know what to do in that situation tells you that the process is broken. The same holds true in the Human Resources side of the dealership. We will dive into our employee handbook later in this chapter, but I think it's important to point out that there should be a page in your employee handbook that addresses what is expected of your employees in regard to personal appearance and what steps will be taken if the appearance of the employees does not meet the standard you have set.

One of the keys to encouraging your employees to maintain a professional appearance is consistency. This begins with you. You are the standard for your people. While that might seem like a lot of pressure, and it is, your people will only be willing to go as far as you push yourself. This holds true for everything that happens in your dealership, not just your professional appearance.

If you don't adhere to what you are asking your people to do, you will be saying one thing and doing another, which will not give your dealership sustainable change. Take time to establish your expectations, communicate them, model them, and reinforce them. You can do this by taking an objective look at your business, and your people, so that your customers will see you as a dealership with premium products and services that are worth the premium investment.

Your Impact on the Community

The impact of your business goes far beyond the walls of your dealership. Whether you are the only employee or you have hundreds of employees, the fact is the same. People need your dealership. They need your products, services, and skills. They need what you offer. The cold, hard truth is that if you were to go out of business, your community would suffer. However, you can't stay in business if you undervalue yourself. By offering a premium product at a premium price point, you are providing an important service to the community. It's not something you should be ashamed of; instead be proud of your achievement, like a boy or girl scout receiving a new merit badge. You wear that "We make our community a better place" badge with pride and celebrate with a s'more!

Products

As the owner or manager of a dealership, you are often viewed as an expert in the product you sell and service, and rightfully so. You know more about the details of the product than just about anyone else. When thinking about conveying professionalism in your dealership and selling your brand, it's important not to undervalue the power of the knowledge.

People Come to Your Business Because You Are the Expert

Think about the amount of time and money you have put into becoming an expert on the products you carry. Okay, this might be as painful as realizing you forgot your anniversary, but really think about it. I assume it's a substantial amount of both time and money. But, if you are like many of our dealers, the product knowledge you and your team have may be one of the best-kept secrets in your dealership!

When you understand that people come to a dealership because you are the experts in the market, it changes how you do things and how you equip your people. Start thinking about how to get the word out. It could be as simple as making sure every invoice leaving your dealership has the cumulative time in the industry of all your employees. Or maybe, list the years of industry experience by department. When your employees finish a certification or training, are you sharing it with your customers? When your customers know about the continued training you are doing with your people, it elevates the status of your dealership in their minds and continues to allow you to charge a premium price for the premium services you offer.

One of our dealers made sure that everyone knew when their service manager completed their EDA Service Manager Certification by not only putting the emblem on their website but by ensuring it was on the dealership's social media accounts and other promotions they sent out.

On the flip side, while you have this incredible knowledge base about the products you carry, your customers don't want *all* of the details about every piece of equipment you have in your dealership. They only want the information that is relevant to them. *Your customers don't need to know everything you know about the product; they just want to know the information that affects them.*

Many times we see salespeople simultaneously talk themselves into and out of a sale because they are oversharing specific product knowledge that the customer just doesn't care about. Your customers only have one question when they are buying from you: "How does this affect me?" The challenge for salespeople is to answer that question with as much clarity as possible while keeping the customer engaged.

We know you have all the information in your head, but not all the information needs to come out of your mouth. Typically, a customer can only retain three key points about a product during their discussion with you or your salesperson. Keep it simple and you will have a customer who not only remains engaged but will be more likely to buy the product or service you're sharing about.

Look Like You Are in Business

If you are going to call yourself a dealer, you need to look like a dealer. Now, to be clear, this doesn't mean that you have the biggest or most expensive building in your area. However, it does mean that regardless of the product you sell, you need to have enough of it on your lot so that you look like you are a serious dealership.

Not long ago, Bob was talking to a dealer we work with about a second store he had opened four years earlier and that had never been profitable. Their primary manufacturer had encouraged him to open a second store to fill a hole they had in the market. Of course, they told him if he didn't do it they would simply find someone else who would, but he was their first choice. The dealer found a location, opened and staffed the store, and spent the next four years losing money. He decided to give Bob a call and ask for some insight. As Bob looked at the numbers of the second location, the amount of money he was losing and his staffing issues, he encouraged the dealer to close down the second dealership and bring all inventory he had back to the primary location. Business has changed; customers don't mind traveling to buy what they want. He had a mobile service that allowed him to take care of customers regardless of where they were. He could ship them parts if they didn't want to come in and they would have them the next day. Bob stressed that while having multiple locations makes your ego swell it does little in most cases to make your bank account swell. As he explained to the dealer, "To get most people to trust you and spend money with you, you have to look like a strong and thriving business. Because of the strain on your floorplan and the resources of trying to have inventory and staffing at both locations, you look like you are barely in business at either place."

Bob used an example of a person who was looking to buy a new truck. He asked the dealer to tell him which of three dealerships the person would probably buy from. The first one was in his town and had ten new trucks on the lot. The second location was thirty minutes away and had thirty new trucks on their lot, and the third location was an hour away that had one hundred new trucks on their lot. The dealer said that the person looking for a new truck would probably drive the hour because the selection was so much better. Bob then asked, "How do you know that the dealer with ten trucks wouldn't have had what he wanted?" The dealer responded that he might, but the perception would be more trucks, more options. "That's exactly right," Bob said. "It wasn't the hour drive, it was the customer's perception that caused him to take the trip to the dealership with more inventory. And that's exactly what I believe you should do. Consolidate your inventory, make your dealership a destination, reduce your expenses, and start making more money."

This is no different from your dealership. If you want to compete, you need to look like you are a stocking and servicing dealer of the brands you carry.

Now, keep in mind that just like not having an adequate supply of inventory, overcrowding also can have a negative effect. No customer wants to squeeze past other units to see the item they are interested in. Give your customers plenty of space to browse by highlighting your products and resist overcrowding your showroom or sales area to that point. Your customers and salespeople need to be able to walk around the products you are selling.

It is also a great idea to take at least one unit and showcase it. Take the top model, with all the bells and whistles, and highlight it. Make sure it's clean and is highlighted in such a way that it draws the customers toward it. This will create a great experience for your customers, elevate your professionalism and image, and help you sell additional features and more product.

Manufacturers and Distributors

We have talked about the important value that your manufacturers and distributors bring to your dealership. They aren't the enemy. Regardless of the person calling on you, whether they are good or bad, they are on your team. You both have the same goal—to sell product and make money. Your manufacturers and distributors aren't trying to ruin your life. They are pushing you, yes, but you are both trying to accomplish the same goal.

I mentioned this in the marketing section, but it's worth bringing it up again. The specific brands you carry (produced by the manufacturers or sold by your distributor) are one of the things that differentiate you from your competitors. Place value on the relationship.

Now, with that in mind, this is still your business. When your manufacturer or distributor's salesperson visits, understand that they are there to help you be successful.

Check your attitude and take action to show them you appreciate how they add value to your business, and work toward making each meeting beneficial.

Keep in mind, both the dealership and the supplier must be successful, which is why the best in the industry value their dealer network above all else.

Setting Labor Rates

When is the last time you raised your labor rate? For most dealers, it's probably been a while. Has the cost of hiring and retaining good employees risen? Have your taxes gone up? What about other expenses? Probably higher than when you initially set your labor rate. But you, as a dealer, feel the need to be benevolent to the community and charge a rate so low, that you end up being the only loser in the situation. Help me understand that. You are the one who takes all the risk, but you are the one who is taking the hit.

When your prices are higher, there is a perceived increased value to the services you offer. Now, if your strategy is that you are going to have the cheapest labor rates in a one-hundred-mile radius, to put out sub-par work and deal with angry customers day in and day out, don't raise your labor rate. However, if you are already putting out quality service, then make sure your labor rate reflects it. Here is what I want you to do. Right before your busiest time of year I want you to raise your labor rate $10 an hour for anyone who hasn't purchased whole goods from you. Here is what's going to happen. You are going to lose the customers who are always pushing you on price (Bye, Felicia!), and the customers you actually like are going to stay. You are going to make up the difference of any "lost" business and you will have additional capacity. So, what's the result? You have to complete less work for the same amount of money, and you get rid of the customers you didn't like in the first place. I think you just won the service jackpot!

Not convinced and want more reasons on why you need a competitive labor rate? I'm glad you asked.

How much does it cost to keep your technicians trained? We all know it is not free. Some of the training can take place online, but even then, you have the hourly cost of the technician, not counting the loss of billable hours they are not producing. If they have to travel for training, then the cost is much greater.

So, you, a benevolent person, are willing to keep investing time and money in your dealership and are just fine with that investment not generating any additional money for you. What would you say to yourself if you were in my place? Probably the same thing I'm getting ready to say to you. This is insanity. But you are so close to the situation that you don't even realize it was an issue until now; and that's okay.

Is this scary, the idea of raising your labor rate? Yes, it is. I get it. You are probably thinking, "What if no one wants me to do their service after this? How will I tell my customers? What will my employees think?" While those are all great questions, from our experience the only one that really becomes the problem is, "What will my employees think?"

In all the years of working with dealers, we've discovered that one of the most common issues is the inability for dealerships to attract and hire great technicians. Great technicians are not difficult to find, but in most cases, they are expensive. The nice thing about a top tech is they can easily pay for themselves, especially if you are using flat rating as a part of your pricing strategy in the shop. The best techs out there can easily produce ten billable hours in an eight-hour day. Your challenge then is to set your labor rate so that you can pay for the talent you want or have.

We currently are working with a dealership who was struggling to find good techs. As Bob was working with Ben and Kay, the owners, he encouraged them to move their labor rate up by $20 per hour so they would be more in-line with their market and have the ability to hire the technicians that would help their service department get back on track.

Both Ben and Kay had the same response that most dealers have: "We can't do that, Bob. None of our customers will do business with us!" Bob explained that they were correct. They could not make an immediate jump from the $70 per hour they were currently charging. However, over the next eighteen months they could make incremental adjustments.

When Bob asked them where their service customers would go if they didn't come to them, they couldn't answer the question. Sure, there were probably a few other places that customers could go, but, if Ben and Kay had better technicians and could quickly produce quality work, wasn't that really what their customers would want?

With the increase in labor rates they could also put a bonus program in place for the service department that would help to eliminate what the employees were thinking—that the owners were just raising the labor rate to be greedy. In the end, Ben and Kay agreed to begin the process of moving their labor rate up, and now, two years later, they are at $95 per hour instead of $70 per hour. They were able to recruit two very good technicians who are pumping out quality work, and they have gained service customers instead of losing them.

Let me walk you through this. Yes, people will want you to keep doing their service. The best time to raise your labor rate is at the busiest time of year when people are focused on quickly getting the serviced unit back, not on how much it's going to cost. And let me add, it doesn't matter what your employees think. They aren't paying your bills.

So, RAISE YOUR STUPID LABOR RATE.

5 Percent Extra on Parts

If you are a dealer (and since you've gotten to this point of the book, I'm guessing you are—pretty sure all of the comedians, politicians, and dog trainers have put it down by now), one thing you need to be doing is adding a minimum of 5 percent to all of the parts you sell to your service department. Why, you might ask? Well, it actually costs you more to sell a part to yourself than it does if a customer walks up to your parts counter.

Think about it this way. When a customer walks up to your parts counter, they typically have the make and model of the product and, in a place where magical unicorns exists, they would also have the serial number. The customer provides the manpower of walking to and from the counter, and they have gathered the basic information on the unit they are needing a part for as well as an educated guess on what they need.

On the flip side, if you are selling a part to yourself through your service department, consider the steps you go through.

- You pay someone to pull the information on the make, model, and serial number.
- You pay someone to figure out what parts are needed, based on the service or repair.
- You pay someone to communicate that information to the parts department.
- You pay someone to transport the parts to the service department.

Unless you are running your dealership as a non-profit organization, you have to recoup the money you are paying out in time and labor somewhere. So, we encourage our dealers to recoup that cost by adding 5 percent to all the parts they sell to themselves. We typically cap this once the cost of a part reaches $100. At that point the extra 5 percent is passed on to the customer.

Do you know how many customers will push back on this 5 percent? Approximately zero. We have been working with thousands of dealers on this for years, and this just doesn't become an issue. We even have a few dealers who have increased their percentage to 11 percent with no customer pushback. Yes, you read that right—11 percent *extra* on parts they sell to themselves.

Now, the logistics of how to do this depends on your dealer management software. Some have made it incredibly easy by simply allowing you to click a button. In other situations, you may have to move your parts pricing at the counter up by the 5 percent and then discount 5 percent back to your counter customers. They will love the extra discount, and it allows us to get the extra 5 percent in the shop that we were looking for.

Here is what we know. Dealers who place a high value on their business and view it as a tool to better serve their customers are more profitable. It's not a bad thing to expect your business to generate money for you.

Many times, the biggest issue you are facing is your attitude toward your dealership. Do you expect it to be the mean, lean, cash-generating machine it can be? What is your attitude toward your people and customers? Do you value the people you have spent time and money to hire and train, as well as the customers who support and trust your business? What about your manufacturers? Are you willing to approach the relationship with a new and improved attitude? The good news is you are in control of both your attitude and the actions you take. You are the solution. Start now to re-mold the perception that others have and take your dealership to a new level of success.

HABIT SIX:

Manage Time Well

I'M THE PROBLEM: *Available 24/7*
I'M THE SOLUTION: *I know when it's "go" time and "no" time.*

I first met April and Dan at a Dealer Association meeting over ten years ago. They had purchased their dealership from a couple who had been a friend of their family. The original owners had built a good business, but with no children to pass it on to and ready to retire, they decided to sell. Dan and April had approached them wanting to buy the business, and sixty days later it was theirs.

Dan was a good mechanic, and April took to the bookkeeping side of the dealership like a fish to water. They were able to hold on to the old customers and worked to continue to grow new ones. Before long, business had doubled.

With the significant increase in growth came more employees, more work, more stress, and less time to get away from the business. To complicate matters, April and Dan were expecting their first child and April was hoping that she could stay at home and work in a part-time capacity at the store.

As we visited, I got a sense from Dan that he felt like they had created a monster and was questioning if they should have tried to keep the dealership small like it had been in the beginning. The growth in business created an increase in both expenses and demands on his time. With the baby due soon, Dan was feeling the pressure. April was visibly upset and felt like she was letting Dan, and their business, down.

I encouraged them both to stay for a while after the meeting so we could talk more and so that maybe I could point them in the right direction. They needed to find a way to create balance between the business and their personal lives.

After the meeting was finished, Dan, April, and I went to the restaurant in the hotel and continued our conversations. I said, "April, you have to stop feeling guilty for wanting to move into a part-time role so you can be at home with your new baby. And Dan, you have to learn how to do a better job managing your time while you are at the dealership so the two of you can have both a great business and a life outside of it."

I told them that for the last several years, they have both spent as much time as needed to get the dealership where it is today. It was their life and that wasn't a bad thing. But now, they were wanting to make some adjustments and needed to begin to wean the business away from requiring all of their time and attention. I said, "Dan, April, you are both going to need to agree to establish some boundaries and be willing to put them into place for both the business and your personal lives."

Continuing, I challenged them, "This is your first child, and you both will quickly learn the importance of setting boundaries for him or her as they grow up. Good boundaries make for a well-mannered, well-behaved child. The same is true for your dealership. One of the first boundaries you will set with your firstborn will have to do with bedtime. Trust me, the sooner you set that boundary, the better your lives will be as parents. You will both need to set time boundaries for your business. How many hours each day and what days of the week will your dealership have access to you as its parents?"

Needing to drive home this all-important message to these parents-to-be, I finished up with, "Another goal you will have for your child is to grow them to a point where they will be able to live on their own without you. The same will be true for your business." With that, I asked them to spend some time on their ride back home and talk about the boundaries they were going to set for the business. We would visit again in a few days so I could continue to walk them through the processes they would need to establish in order to make the dealership self-sufficient.

On the following Tuesday, I got a call from April. She and Dan had a great conversation on their ride home and were ready to get started creating the boundaries we had talked about. With that, I asked what they had decided. She said that Dan was going to be at the dealership Monday through Friday at 7 a.m. and had committed to being home at 6 p.m. each night. On Saturday he was going to go in at 7:30 and leave no later than 12:30 during season. When season was done, he was going to be in the store every other Saturday and switch off with his parts person, Jesse. "That's a great plan," I assured April.

"So April, how about you?" I asked. April said, "I am going to go in after lunch for two hours a day and take the baby with me. It should be nap time for him and I can get everything I need done. We talked to our accountant and she is going to handle a lot of the bookkeeping I was doing before."

"That is a great first plan," I said. "So let's see if we can make it happen before the baby gets here. Starting on Monday of next week, I want you both to commit to me that you will follow the boundaries you have set, and let's see what happens."

Curious to see how it was going, I called them the following week on Wednesday afternoon at 3:00. April answered the phone. "April," I said, "I'm a little surprised you answered the phone. It's three o'clock, you should be gone by now. What happened?"

"I'm finding it hard to get away like I had hoped; it just seems that once I come in there are so many things I need to do, and I can't keep up," April said.

"Has your accountant started helping you yet?" I asked.

"No, I haven't had a chance to meet with her."

"Haven't had a chance, or haven't taken the time?" I asked.

April laughed and said, "I haven't taken the time." As we talked more, I impressed upon April that if she was going to make this work, she would have to take time to do what was important now so later she would have time to deal with the urgent things that were sure to come up. I asked her to have Dan give me a call so we could catch up.

I found out later that Dan was struggling with the same issues April was facing. I made them both promise that they would restart next week and commit to getting those time boundaries set. It ended up taking about three weeks of me hounding them, but they finally got into the rhythm and things were moving along pretty well. April's accountant had taken on the tasks that April needed done, and Dan was working with Jesse, his parts person, and breaking up some of Dan's load so he could get out on time.

That was over ten years ago. Now Dan and April have three children, two boys and a girl. Their business has continued to grow and prosper. Over those ten years, both Dan and April have become masters at managing their boundaries and creating a balance between the business and their personal lives. Jesse is now the parts manager who oversees both their in-store parts sales as well as their online parts sales, grossing over $1 million per year. All three of the children are in sports. Dan coaches two youth baseball teams and makes it to his daughter's weekly soccer games.

I think the most important thing to remember about April and Dan was their commitment to creating a life balance between the business and their family. Over the years, Dan stopped reacting to what was happening around him and became proactive. He became more of a coach than a manager to his people and better communicated what his needs and expectations were of his employees. He established strong processes in each department and grew his department managers so that they could not only effectively run their own department but also cross over or help if others needed it. When a problem or issue came up that the managers needed Dan's help on, he dealt with it immediately rather than putting it off and then required the department manager to adjust the process so they wouldn't have to deal with it again. The story that Bob just shared with Dan and April is not unique in the world of dealerships, their commitment and follow-through on creating life balance is a habit of a successful dealer.

CHOOSE YOUR SUPERPOWER

If I could grant you a superpower, what would you choose? Maybe invisibility? The ability to teleport anywhere in the world? The power to fly? Just like in the story Bob told, you, like Dan and April, might choose the ability to stop time.

I've never met a dealership owner or manager who hasn't had a constant need for more time. Every owner or manager I visit with is typically juggling what seems like hundreds of things at once, while trying to maintain some semblance of sanity. At the end of the day, when the doors are locked and we have finally made it home, most everyone can relate to one overwhelming feeling: exhaustion. Exhaustion from constantly fighting battles. Exhaustion from being the best salesperson, technician, or parts person. "Doing it all" while trying to run and grow the business.

One of the things that differentiates dealers who run successful and profitable dealerships from dealers who constantly struggle to survive is that they have made an important decision. They have decided they no longer will ride the proverbial roller coaster, and they manage their time in a way that allows them to control the trajectory of their lives and their business.

Before we get too far into this habit, I think there are two things we must address. First, to those of you who already possess a magical formula allowing you to plan every minute of your day and unlock your productive potential to its fullest, I'm happy for you, I really am. But I know for the rest of you, there is an overwhelming pull on your time. As soon as you enter the door, your role changes from manager to firefighter. Even the best-planned day can be flipped on its head in a single moment by a customer, employee, or manufacturer issue.

Second, the thing we need to agree on is this. The idea of achieving total work-life balance is insanity. The idea that one can achieve "work-life balance" is one of the most ridiculous and unrealistic concepts ever sold to mankind, and the pursuit of the "perfect" formula will only drive you crazier. I'm a firm believer that you go through seasons (literally and figuratively). Some seasons will require more of your attention at the dealership, while others might allow you to direct more attention toward home, and neither of those is bad. They can coexist. Now, with that in mind, let's talk about how successful and profitable dealers manage their time.

Clear Goals Help to Direct Your Time

In Habit One, we talked about the importance of mission, core values, and vision in your dealership. Now, I know you probably remember that chapter word for word but, just in case you need a refresher, let me remind you. Your mission is who you always are, regardless. This doesn't change. Your vision is where you are trying to go. Your core values are your personal guidelines on how you will achieve your mission and vision. If you want to run a successful and profitable dealership, everything must come back to your vision. You have to ask yourself every day, "What do I need to do to achieve our vision?" However you answer is where you need to invest your time, energy, and resources. Everything else is simply background noise to your greater focus. When you lose sight of your vision (see what I did there), you enter into a downward spiral, allowing the business to happen to you instead of you happening to it.

Good Time Management Comes from Establishing and Maintaining Strong Boundaries

Dealers who successfully control their time didn't just wake up one day and realize they had become magically blessed and equipped with the ability to control their time. No. They, like you, had to work at developing this skill. The best news about a skill? It can be learned, practiced, and refined. The worst news about a skill? It has to be learned, practiced, and refined. But, the more time and effort you put into it, the better you will get.

Your Priorities Dictate Your Boundaries

Great time managers know that boundaries are the building blocks of time management. Now, I'm not going to start reciting Dr. Henry Cloud, author of the book *Boundaries*, but what is important to remember is that your priorities, either spoken or unspoken, dictate boundaries. If that's true, what does that say about your priorities now? What needs to change for you to ensure that where you are spending your time is in agreement with the future you envision? When you take a radical and honest look at your priorities, you will find that boundaries will follow, and your time will be directed as a result.

Let's say, for example, one of your priorities is being present at dinner with your family every night. You know that your family will be around the table at 6:30. If it's truly a priority for you, you will put boundaries in place and manage your time in a way that allows you to be there. Your boundary might be not taking any calls after 5:30 so you can be out the door by 6:00. You will make time, and be on time, if it is important to you.

Maybe you are like Dan, from the story at the beginning who is now a baseball coach for his two sons. Do you know where you can find him at 4:00 every afternoon during baseball season? Not at the dealership. He has put boundaries in place so that his role as the owner of the dealership will not interfere with his commitment during the baseball season, and he sticks with it.

The best news about boundaries is that you get to decide what they are and how they are put into place. And, if they matter to you as much as you say, you will manage time in a way that you never thought possible, all for the sake of respecting your priorities. To put it simply, your time management (or lack of it) is a direct reflection of the boundaries you put in place to protect your goals, priorities, and vision.

Don't Let Your Dealership Become the Thirty-Year-Old Child Living in Your Basement

More often than not, dealers view their business as the thirty-year-old child living in the basement who spends the entire day playing video games. The dealer thinks, "This is all it will ever be; this is as good as it gets." While that may be true about your business right now, let's expect more of your dealership, your people, and yourself. Expect your business to look for new customers when things start slowing down (whattt?!). Expect your employees to wake up every day with a sense of purpose (your vision). And, expect the business to start paying the rent! When you put these boundaries and expectations in place, you can move your dealership from the child in the basement to the neurosurgeon that his parents always dreamed he could be. Okay, maybe that's a stretch, but I do know that in either situation your thirty-year-old child and your dealership are both capable of so much more.

You Need to Teach Your People How to Manage Their Time

Regardless of your situation, your people look to you as an example and guide when it comes to time management. Just like modeling the dress code, you set the precedent on how we manage and treat the time that is spent at work. If you show up every day in cut-off shorts and a beat-up T-shirt, your people will assume that's the standard of appearance. Do you have a manager in your dealership who shows up "on his time" every day and you do nothing about it because you want to avoid a major blowup? Your people will assume that the behavior is acceptable. Do you ever take real vacation time away from the dealership? If not, your people will assume that you do not mean it when you say time off is important, or they will infer that taking time off would reflect negatively on them because it's not something you do.

How do you do this? By practicing what you preach. By not leading through empty threats but instead showing them how it's done and enforcing what you have set as the standard. While this may not be on your "top 10 things that bring me overwhelming joy" list, know this: whatever you don't address you allow. By simply addressing the issue you become the solution to this problem.

The challenging part of this whole uncomfortable situation is that you are the only solution, and if you decide to take back control of your dealership, it applies to everything inside your dealership.

- *The tech who is holding you hostage.* If you don't establish strong boundaries that allow you to deal with him or her, you are allowing the behavior.

- *The irate customer who comes into the dealership and shares his strongly worded thoughts with the parts department.* This isn't therapy; if you don't address it, you are allowing it.
- *The salesperson who spends the entire day "researching" and whose sales are lacking because of his inactivity.* If you don't address it, you are allowing it.
- *The family member who walks in and takes everyone's focus off the job they are doing.* If you don't address it, you are allowing it. (Sorry, Dad, we need to chat!)

The same holds true for the positive things that are happening. If you have a strong focus on growth, your people will rise to that level if they are trained, equipped, and encouraged, or they will leave.

Let's say you have employees who decide to quit because you increase your expectations and strengthen boundaries. What should you do? Let's throw them a party, with margaritas, good music, and food from the best pizza joint down the road. We are celebrating! This person isn't a good fit, and a "bon voyage" best-of-luck-to-you party is the way to celebrate. I also want you to give them a referral to the dealership down the road. While there might be momentary pain in losing an employee, it will be fleeting because you will have more time and capacity to grow the people on your team, as well as the new ones you hire, who will move your dealership forward.

A few years ago, I started a daily habit of writing down a few things I am thankful for and then listing some of my big goals. It is a small, but quick way to not only keep me grounded but also keep me focused. I thought nothing of it until one day I looked over and saw one of my eight-year-old daughters with an open journal, writing down what she was thankful for and her goals. Had I ever explicitly told her what I was writing in my journal? No, but just like your people with you, she is always watching and taking her cues from me.

So, how do you begin to manage your own personal time well and in a way that shows your people what you expect of them? Let's start with the one-hour challenge.

THE ONE-HOUR CHALLENGE

If you had one hour a day that you weren't interrupted, what could you accomplish? Almost anything, right? I want you to pick something that is important to helping you achieve the vision you have set out for your dealership, and commit one solid hour a day for the next week and work on it.

For example, if you're wanting to create stability in your dealership, your one hour (or power hour, you can call it whatever you want!) may be focused on forecasting and establishing a budget, by department, for the coming year. If your focus is growth, maybe that hour is spent diving into the marketing plan. Everyone's "one thing" is different, but your "one thing" that you invest a dedicated hour each day on will move your dealership toward your vision. Just pick one thing that will allow you to move toward your vision.

Like I mentioned, I'm asking you to commit one uninterrupted hour a day for one week. However, with that in mind, I want you to make it your best hour. This means when your brain is fresh and you are ready to think and work. Are you a morning person or an afternoon person? If you have an afternoon slump, after lunch, that is not the time for your hour. You will just end up on your phone playing games (speaking from experience). So, if you're a morning person, make your hour the first hour of the day. If you're not a morning person, don't do that, but find the time you are most alert and ready to get to work.

At this point, shut your door and tell your people that unless 911 has to be called, they cannot bother you for the next hour. Guess what? Everyone will survive for one hour each day without you. If a problem comes up, they will either figure it out or they will wait, and you will have held an important boundary. Way to go!

So, pick your one thing and get to work.

Are you needing a little more guidance on where to start? Here's what I want you to do.

Write the name of each department represented in your dealership and the words "Stability," "Growth," and "Accountability" under each department.

For each department that didn't generate a profit last year I want you to circle the word "Stability." Like we talked about in Habit Four, if what you are doing isn't making you money, you need to either stop doing it or figure out how to make money doing it.

If you circled "Stability" under any of the departments, this is where you need to begin making changes and where you need to spend your hour. There are several things you can do to begin to create stability, but to get you started we will outline at least one suggestion per department.

Keep in mind, as you read through these suggestions, I don't expect you to tackle all of these today. If you did, you probably wouldn't do any of them well, which will only leave you frustrated and yelling at the book. Pick one item and use your entire one hour of time a day, every day, until it gets done. Then, and only then, do I want you to move on to the next one. My guess is that you, like many entrepreneurs, have a list of great ideas and projects you have started but never finished because something else that was shiny and exciting caught your eye. If you want to be the solution, you need to pick one item in one department and commit to spending your hour on it, until it's completed.

Stability

Service: When working to achieve stability in the service department, the goal of most dealerships is to measure the right numbers. In order to get the right numbers, you must have the right data. This starts with your technicians clocking in and out of work orders. Yes, there are other numbers you should be looking at, but everything is built on your technicians' time.

Parts: As you think about parts, start with your margins. Your target margin will vary based upon the equipment you carry, but all the targets should be at or above MSRP unless you have handpicked them as lost leaders so you can draw people in who will then buy more expensive parts. Don't forget that MSRP is a suggestion and determined by turning a part four times a year. If a part is turning less than four times, the part's price should be above MSRP.

We also detailed how to use both matrix and velocity pricing in Habit Two to improve your margins. If you need a refresher, turn back when you finish this chapter and go reread through the process of implementing them into your parts-pricing strategy.

Sales: Stability in sales begins by measuring the activity of your salespeople. We require every salesperson to make a minimum of twenty touches a day. This could be a phone call, email, or someone walking in your door.

Growth

Now, as you look at your paper, identify which department has the potential for growth. In order for sustained growth to occur, the department needs to be stable first. Yes, you can have growth in a department, but a lack of stability will make it a never-ending nightmare for you. So, which departments are ready for growth? Here are suggestions, by department, that can help you generate growth.

Service: Growth often happens when the people you have are being utilized to their full potential. This can happen if you bring on a service coordinator or roll out a compensation plan based upon efficiency for your technicians.

Parts: Growth in parts occurs by providing training for your parts people, helping them to become parts salespeople, and teaching them skills such as upselling and cross-selling. By implementing upselling and cross-selling, this alone can produce growth up to 35 percent in the parts department!

Sales: The key to growth in whole goods is having a marketing plan that mimics how and when you need increased sales. If you know that 20 percent of whole goods sales happen in April, you need to be spending 20 percent of your marketing budget four to six weeks before you expect to see the sales occur.

Accountability

The last category is "Accountability." Look at the departments you've listed and ask yourself, "Are there any departments that have achieved stability and growth?" If the answer is yes, it's time to set accountability goals for the department.

Service: For the service department you might begin by having regular meetings with your team to share numbers and financials. When your entire team is aware of the common goals and what needs to happen in order to achieve them, it creates accountability for both them and you.

Parts: In this area, you may need to develop a plan to burn down your parts inventory at the peak of season. This accountability frees up cash flow during the slow season but also gives you the ability to place orders with your manufacturers in a way that gives you the best possible discounts.

Sales: For many of our dealers, a goal of sales accountability is an intense focus on the little things. This can be as simple as making sure all customer information is inputted into your CRM. This is often one of the things that salespeople can get lazy on, and its effects are wide-reaching.

While each one of your departments may be at a different point of maturity in your dealership, it's important to keep in mind that you must start with one thing. Your first focus should be to get each department to a place of stability, and from there you can determine a plan for growth and accountability.

A healthy and profitable business is powered by healthy and profitable departments. Taking a one-hour challenge every day will allow you to move your dealership to a place of you running it instead of it running you.

As I mentioned before, when you start modeling good time management, your team will begin to mimic those same behaviors. You might start seeing your service manager set an hour aside each day to work on warranties, or your parts manager may invest dedicated time on fine-tuning margins, and your sales manager may develop a cohesive marketing plan that lines up with your forecasting for the next year. The first step is for you to create the boundary, the example, and set this time aside for you to focus on your business and nothing else.

People who are good time managers are good at saying no, and that takes practice. Honestly, this is easiest if you are the grinch and have a heart that is two sizes too small, but the clearer your boundaries, the easier it will be to stick to your guns and protect your time. At the end of the day, you are the solution to your time management problems. It's up to you to manage your time in a way that will help move your dealership toward your vision.

The hardest part of setting boundaries is sticking to them. Especially the first time. Every time you say no, it just gets a little bit easier. When the people around you know you are serious about the boundaries you have set, something incredible starts to happen. They will start supporting you and respecting your boundaries. Now, at first, they are going to push you. They want to see if you mean what you say (that's called integrity), but as you remain consistent over time, they will call you out when you start to slide on a boundary you have set.

It's not lost on me how difficult it can be to say no, especially if it isn't something you are used to. So, I've compiled a number of ways to say no. Ready? Here we go. You might want to take notes!

1. "No." (Yes, "no" is a full sentence.)
2. "I've got a lot on my plate right now. Is there anyone else who might be able to give this the attention it deserves?" (Or you can even simply point them in the right direction.)
3. "I wish I could, but I can't."
4. "I am not available." Or, "I have other commitments, so no, I can't."
5. "Nope" (this works as a full sentence too!), "Nada," and "Sorry, not sorry" are appropriate responses too.

While you are developing the habit of saying no, it will be uncomfortable at first. The clearer you are on what you are trying to accomplish (your vision), the easier it will be to say no to those things that take you away from what you are trying to achieve. Anything that pulls you away from that is a time vampire, sucking whatever precious time it can and not producing the results you need.

CHAOS COSTS YOU MONEY

Boundaries are a critical step in time management. They allow you to decide what is and isn't important for yourself and your dealership. Dealerships who have perpetually terrible time management and can never get in front of this issue end up one of two ways—burnt out or broke. Typically, they end up both. This happens because, in your business, lack of time management (or chaos) costs you your money and sanity.

So, how does someone get out of this merry-go-round from hell? It starts by having good processes in place. Now, if your first response is "My people will never go for processes," then either you need to change the people or you need to change the people. Noticing a theme? How you run your business is not up to your employees. I don't care if Uncle Billy has been at the parts department for thirty years. It's not Uncle Billy's money or sanity you are losing; it's yours.

It's also important to realize that you already have processes in place; they might just be bad ones.

Bad Service Processes:
- Calling the customer back, only after they have called multiple times about their unit
- Looking at the product for the first time when your technician is ready to work on it
- Allowing your technicians to look up and pull their own parts

Bad Parts Processes:
- Dealing with the stocking order when you "have time"
- Blaming a forgotten parts order on either a back order or the manufacturer

Bad Sales Processes:
- Keeping all the customer information in your head
- Marketing only when business starts to slow down

How do you know you have a bad process or a breakdown in process? It's when you become the process. When your people come to you and ask you how to handle a situation, that means there is a breakdown in processes.

We hear it all the time. "I don't need to write down the processes, I have them all in my head." Or, "It's really not that complicated." If you want to reclaim your time and begin to move away from the burnt-out and broke stage, this has to change. I appreciate the fact that you know all of the processes. I'll even give you a high-five if we ever meet. But what happens to the dealership, to your people, and to your customers if something happens and you can't be at work for an extended period of time? Or look at it this way: Could you imagine what it would be like if you weren't interrupted every few minutes with another question that could have been easily answered by a written process? For most owners and managers, it would be an incredible shift in reclaiming the time in your dealership.

We need to move from a place of reactionary time management to proactive time management.

Reactionary time management typically happens by default. A customer calls in and is upset, so we react. A tech shows up an hour late, again. We react. The stocking order didn't get put away when it came in and we are missing parts, so we react. Reactionary time management is an exhausting place to be. It creates unrealistic demands on you that will dictate how you spend your time and money. Just to be clear, we are taking control of our sanity, our life, and our dealership, and to do this, it means that the only person who is dictating where your time goes in a day is you.

Let's say that you head to the local gas station to fill up your car. While at the gas station, the person at the pump next to yours decides they will be the one to tell you how much fuel you should put in your truck, what kind of fuel, and how you will pay for it.

You would never let that happen, probably for many reasons, but the main one is that the person at the next pump doesn't have all of the information. They don't know if your truck uses flex fuel, regular, premium, or diesel fuel. They don't know where you need to go or how much money you have to pay for it.

The same is true with your time. Don't let the customer or employee who doesn't have all of the information be the one who dictates how you run your dealership or your life. It is possible to move from a day full of reactionary time management to one that is focused on proactive time management.

Reactionary is what we default to when we are trying to deal with chaos. Proactive allows us to manage and direct the chaos. How this plays out in each department is a little different, but moving to a proactive approach will save you valuable time and money.

REACTIVE VERSUS PROACTIVE IN SERVICE

Raise your hand (or your pen, or your drink) if you have ever been the recipient of what seems like an unending cycle of calls from customers who seem to have a chip on their shoulder and are targeting you as the person to unleash their furry on? Oh, all of you? In service, we have to move from a place of letting our customers dictate how our time is spent, to setting up systems that meet their needs and yours.

Triaging Units

If there was one secret weapon that could fix the bulk of the problems in your service department, would you want to know what it is? Well, the secret weapon is the process of triaging. When implementing our processes, one of the key elements, if not the key element, in getting your service department to start producing obscene amounts of money, is a process called triaging.

Think about triaging in terms of what happens with paramedics at an accident site. When an ambulance pulls up, they quickly check the status of everyone involved and then start communicating with the hospital about what will be coming into the emergency room. I want you to take this same mentality with the units that come in for repair. Your goal is twofold—a quick diagnosis and clear communication.

In your service department, during the hour before lunch and/or the hour before the end of the day, line up all of the units that have come in that day and have the technician who will be working on that unit, and the service coordinator if you have one, evaluate it. This is not a long, in-depth diagnostic. This is a quick look that allows the technician to do a visual, start a parts order, and give the service manager some information on what they suspect the issue is and how long it will take to fix it. This allows the service manager to communicate to the customer and receive the go-ahead, if needed. Then, once that is done, the parts department can begin to pull or order the parts, allowing the repair to be scheduled in the next one to four days.

During the slower times of the year, this is something you should do once a day. While in peak season, you should be triaging all units twice a day.

Triaging should happen an hour before lunch or an hour before the end of a day for a very specific reason—because people want to go somewhere else. They either want to leave and eat or leave and go home; the efficiency you get from your people at these two times of the day is second to none. It also allows technicians to leave on a positive note. If your technicians leave in a bad mood, how will they be when they come back into the dealership the next day? Probably in a similar mood. Scheduling the triage time at the end of the day allows them to wrap the day up with a victory.

Do you remember the painful but oh so rewarding process of cleaning up all of the crap in the service department that we talked about in Habit Two? We want to make sure the mess doesn't come back in. This includes dirt. Because of this, every unit should be cleaned before it comes in for triage unless there is an oil leak. This allows the shop to stay clean and your technicians to give you the most accurate estimate on the scope of the repair. The triage process helps you better manage the time of the technicians and parts people and allows you to be proactive, instead of reactive, in reaching out to customers about the status of their unit.

Communication Plans

Another process that may seem unimportant in the service department, but will allow you and your team to be proactive in the management of time and reduce chaos, is establishing a good communication plan. *Oh heavens. Not a communication plan.* Here's the thing. In a dealership, the complexity, especially in the service department, demands that you become a master juggler. A service manager must be able to communicate with technicians, customers, the parts department, the sales department, and the owner or GM, often regarding the same service or repair. If just reading that last sentence caused you to be overcome with fear, it's time for a better plan. Having a proactive plan on how to communicate with each person, or group of people, can change your day drastically.

COMMUNICATING WITH TECHNICIANS

When communicating with technicians, find one time, typically at the end of the day, to bring your technicians together and talk about what is in line for them the next day. When scheduling the next day's work, you want to put the hardest job first and tell them about it before they leave. This allows them to start thinking about it that evening and come in with it on their mind the next day. Besides, who doesn't like to start their day knowing what is ahead?

COMMUNICATING WITH CUSTOMERS

I know, to you, it may seem like you are barraged with an endless slew of customer phone calls in the service department, people just wanting to "check on" their unit to see when they can come pick it up. By having a process and communicating it with the customers when they drop the units off at the service department, you will begin to take control. Many of our dealers, depending on product mix, tell the customer that they will reach back out to them within twenty-four hours (this is where triage helps!) with an update or estimate. Then they actually do it! This could be through text message, phone call, email, or a combination of all three. Service managers find that this reduces the number of random calls from customers looking for an update, saving them time and effort.

If you weren't constantly fielding calls from customers asking about the status of their unit, what amount of time would you gain back into your day? At least an hour? Maybe more? Being proactive in communicating with your customers will eliminate a large amount of chaos in your service department.

COMMUNICATING WITH YOUR PARTS PEOPLE

If you are a service manager, I would encourage you to visit once a day with the parts manager about the parts you will probably need for upcoming service and repairs. This will allow them to get the parts moving in your direction. There is no need for the service and parts departments to be mortal enemies. You are both trying to do the same thing: provide the best possible service to your customers. You may have different ways of accomplishing that goal, and that's okay. However, a quick meeting, once a day, ideally about an hour before the stocking order is placed, will go a long way in saving both departments time, money, and frustration. You might even realize that the parts manager isn't so bad after all and be able to decrease the constant level of anxiety you have previously brought to each other's lives.

COMMUNICATING WITH THE SALES DEPARTMENT

When it comes to sales, we always plan a certain amount of "emergency" time for the sales department. What if they need a miracle in order to close a sale? You need to be able to come along and help them without causing chaos in your department. This is done by planning a minimum of one hour of emergency time into every day, per technician. Other uses of emergency time might include assembling a new unit, getting a rental unit back to rentable condition, or even a customer emergency. If you don't end up needing the time, you simply move the next job in line into the spot. But again, at the end of each day, I encourage you to ask the sales manager about anything they may see coming down the pipeline, even if it's not a done deal, so you can plan accordingly.

REACTIVE VERSUS PROACTIVE
IN PARTS

It's probably not lost on you that being proactive managers of time in the parts department is hard. I don't know if your customers are all just standing together, outside and around the corner waiting for that perfect moment when they yell "now!" and come running through your door. It seems they all need their part at the same moment. Many parts managers will tell you this is exactly what it seems like! Because of the uncertainty of customer demand, processes are the only way to be proactive in parts.

Special and Emergency Parts Orders

If there is one thing that can throw a parts department into chaos, it's a customer who ordered a special or emergency order that can't be found. So, what's your process for dealing with special and emergency or unit down parts orders? If your parts department is like most, there may not be one. First, just to clarify, special orders are orders from customers who need a part that you don't typically carry in your inventory. Emergency or unit down orders generally come from your service department, and sometimes A-level customers, and are typically needed by 10 a.m. the next morning.

If a customer comes in with a special order, you are going to do a few things. First, require payment upfront. Seriously, go look in your parts department right now. Do you have a shelf of "parts of repairs past" that is full of special orders? The ones where the customer never came back in to get them? Probably. You don't want their indecisiveness to eat into your margins. The way you do that is to make sure to collect the money upfront for both the part and the freight costs. Your goal is that your freight account remains neutral. The way most dealers have success with this is by charging a flat fee, based on either part price or weight.

When the parts come in, you need to put them in a special bin, a dedicated area of your parts department, and organized by the first letter of the customers' last name. This will help save time and reduce chaos when the parts arrive. You also need to make sure to communicate with the customer as soon as the part comes in. How you do that is up to you, but make sure you let your customers know how you will be in touch and when they can most likely expect the part.

Now, with an emergency or unit down order from the service department or an A-level customer, there is never going to be a time that you are going to tell them no. If they need a part overnighted, we are going to overnight the part. That's it. Let's say that the service department is in the middle of a job, and the unit is torn apart and taking up valuable space. In the middle of the repair, they realize that they needed an additional part to finish the job. If this is a low-dollar part, you may not feel like you can justify the cost of overnighting it. Just to be clear, this decision is not up to you. What you might not see is that this low-dollar part is what is standing between the shop's ability to wrap up a large, lucrative repair. The $12.99 overnight shipping cost is nothing in comparison to getting this $5,000 job completed and out the door. Plus, the additional freight can be built into the cost of the repair.

When you have an emergency or unit down order, keep in mind, just like with a customer, your service department needs to be communicated with as soon as it comes in. They would not have you overnight if it was something that could have waited.

Take the time to identify and lay out your process, and how you will communicate it to anyone who is working behind the parts counter.

"Hoping" Inventory Stays Correct

Another giant chaos creator in parts is not having a process for inventory control.

The best and easy(ish) way to make sure that you are being proactive managers of time and maintaining the integrity of the parts department is by not letting techs pull their own parts.

We all know that the greatest disruptor of an accurate parts inventory is not actually your parts people; it's the technicians. Now, the technicians don't come in and hope that they can ruin your life or mess up integrity of your inventory, but both things seem to happen almost simultaneously the moment they pass the imaginary boundary that should protect the parts department.

Most of the time, technicians are just focused on getting the part they need to get their job done, but in the midst of the noble pursuit, they cause chaos. They might forget to add the part to their work order and create high levels of stress for others that will have to be worked through with their therapist.

To be proactive, there are two things you can do to reclaim your parts department's inventory integrity. First, never let anyone who isn't a parts person behind the counter. That's right. The parts department is a bank vault full of one-hundred-dollar bills. You wouldn't let just anyone into a bank vault, and you're not going to let just anyone into the parts department.

Second, I want you to consider hiring a part-time person (we call them the parts support specialist) whose salary will be offset by the extra 5 percent you charge the service department on parts you sell to them. This person is going to account for and put away all stocking orders that come in, pull parts for techs, and make sure the parts that the service department are buying are added to work orders. This person eliminates chaos and saves money.

REACTIVE VERSUS PROACTIVE IN SALES

Have you noticed what separates mediocre salespeople from incredible ones? Hint, it has to do with this chapter. They are proactive in the way they manage their time, and they understand that the way to produce more sales is to make sure that every minute of their working time is used to interact and engage with customers. So where do you start if you or some of your employees have developed bad habits in sales?

Marketing When Things Are Slow

We talked a little about this earlier, but just in case you skimmed it before, it's worth mentioning again. Your marketing should take place four to six weeks ahead of when you need to see an increase in sales and customer traffic. So often we see dealerships fall into the cycle of "We need sales now. Let's start putting money into marketing." You "hope" that the money you have thrown out into the universe will come back to you with quick, high-dollar sales. Hope is not a marketing strategy I can get behind. Once you throw this money toward marketing, on the basis of hope, you get frustrated by the fact that the marketing "isn't working." Marketing works best when you are proactive in planning and determining how and where you spend your money. A well-executed marketing plan will reduce chaos, while saving you frustration and money.

Waiting for Leads to Come In

One of the most reactionary things that salespeople do is to wait for leads to come in. If you want your salespeople to generate consistent revenue, they have to embrace the fact that your dealership has the premium phone plan. You know, the one that not only allows calls to come in but also allows your employees to make outbound calls as well. I'll give you a minute to verify that this is the plan you have.

If your salespeople are simply waiting for the next sale to happen, they have simply become order takers and reactionary managers of their time, and you need to give them a project. Using your CRM, pull a list of customers who have purchased from you in the last five to seven years. Ask your salespeople to start calling through the list. The five-to-seven-year customer window is an important one to pay attention to. In that time frame, a few things have probably happened. If the customer financed the product, it's typically paid off, the warranty is probably expired, and most consumers are ready for something new. It sounds like the perfect scenario to make new sales.

Give your salespeople this list of past customers and have them call to simply check in with them. This is not a hard sales call but a "just touching base" call.

This is also a great place to start with a new salesperson. We were working with a tractor dealership years ago who had just hired David for inside sales. We told David to pull the list of customers who bought from them over the past five to seven years using their CRM. We then told him to start calling and introducing himself. We had him say, "Hi, my name is David from ABC Dealership and I'm new here. The owner, Steve, wanted me to call and introduce myself and see if there was anything we could do to help." Using that list and the power of picking up the phone, David generated over $1 million in tractor sales in his first year at the dealership.

Would he have had the same success if he had taken a reactionary, wait-until-they-walked-through-the-door approach? Probably not.

REACTIVE VERSUS PROACTIVE WITH YOUR PEOPLE

Let's talk about how you manage your time with your people. If issues are not addressed in a proactive way, they can easily become one of the largest time drains to you. As an owner or manager, you have the ability to move from reacting to the (what seems like a non-stop) parade of employee issues to getting in front of them before they explode and you have to clean up the mess, which is not good for anyone at the dealership.

Dealing with Issues When They Erupt

It can be easy to sweep employee issues under the rug until they become a big issue that affects everyone in the dealership. I get it; it's not fun to deal with, but, like a leak in your roof, the issue will just get worse until you eventually fix it. Employee issues won't fix themselves.

The two best tools you can use are the humble employee review and the employee handbook. I know, let's all groan collectively.

The employee review or performance review allows you to see how the employee thinks he or she is doing versus how you think they are doing.

There are three things owners and managers need to keep in mind during a performance review:

1. Even if you are getting ready to give a positive performance review, your employee is going to be nervous.

Before you walk into the performance review, put yourself in your employee's shoes. We often encourage owners and managers to take their employees to a coffee shop or a meal outside of the dealership for their performance review. At the very least, try to provide a private setting. This may mean scheduling the thirty-minute review before or after hours. It tends to reduce their stress level down and lead to a more open and honest conversation.

2. The performance review should never be the first time an employee hears about a problem from you.

If there is an issue with one of your employees, it is vitally important that you address it quickly and efficiently when you discover it. As a parent, if I wanted one of my kids to start making their bed on a daily basis, I would need to address it immediately and daily. It wouldn't be something that I kept a tally of over a six-month time period and then presented to them logically at the end of the year. That wouldn't change the behavior for my kids, and it won't change the behavior of your employees.

3. You have to spend time preparing for the review.

Yes, performance reviews take time, but the results are well worth it. We encourage all the dealerships we work with to perform what we call "360 reviews." These are reviews done by both the manager and the employee in order to see any differences in understanding about how things are going.

Taking time to conduct reviews twice a year will allow you to move to a place of being proactive with employee issues instead of just reacting to the problem when it finally becomes unbearable. Over time, these will get easier for both you and your people.

Employee Handbook

Your employee handbook, put simply, is your HR process for your dealership. Here are a few things you should keep in mind when putting together an employee handbook.

1. An employee handbook speaks for you.

An employee handbook gives your employees answers to the questions they might have about things such as time off, dress codes, acceptable behavior, and discipline policies, before they are even asked. Remember, if you receive a specific question more than once, there is a breakdown in your processes that will cause chaos and suck both time and money from your business. Once you get the same question twice, go back and update the process (in this case the employee handbook) and make sure that everyone is updated on the change.

2. One size can fit all.

If your employee handbook is thorough enough, it isn't necessary to have a separate handbook for each department. This can save you time, overall, in explaining policies and expectations from department to department.

3. Expectations are clear.

You should make sure that you have at least a basic job description and clear expectations for each position in the dealership, which feed into the policies outlined in the employee handbook.

4. Establish guidelines from day one.

Each new employee should be given the handbook before they start the job, with the expectation that they will sign off on each page to show they have read and understand what the expectations of the dealership are on the day they start the job.

5. You can modify behavior and expectations annually.

At least once a year you should review your handbook, make changes based upon any behavior you want to encourage or change, and update the handbook accordingly. Then, present employees with the new or revised handbook. At the time the employees are given the updated handbook, they should be asked to sign off on the changes and are then held accountable to the standards outlined in the handbook.

• • •

Keep in mind, your business is a vehicle that leads you to the life you want to live; it is not your life. Honestly, it's easy to get this backward. Often, your business becomes your entire life. In those moments, when your boundaries are nonexistent or you are guarding the wrong thing, you are on the road to burnout, not only for yourself but for your family and those close to you. But the good news? This is something you can control. You can regain control of your life and your dealership. Identifying this as a problem is the first step to taking back your time, your sanity, and your money. As you start flexing your time management muscles, the people around you will notice, and begin to do the same. It's up to you to start this movement inside of your dealership. Why not start today?

HABIT SEVEN:

Hire the Right People for the Team

I'M THE PROBLEM: *Where did I get THESE people?*
I'M THE SOLUTION: *I'm coaching my team to win it all.*

Jackie called into our offices to find out what kind of hiring tools we might have to help her do a better job in hiring and retaining people. Jackie worked for her dad, Matt. She had graduated college with a business degree and, with coaxing from her dad, decided to come work for the business and was currently running the HR department.

As I spoke with her, we learned more about their business. What had started out as a single-store operation twenty-five years ago had now grown into four locations with almost fifty full-time employees and, from Jackie's perspective, their employee issues were contributing to financial stress on the dealerships as well as morale problems that were beginning to impact their customers.

As we talked about the assessments and their business, she began to tell me more about her father, Matt, the business, and what she saw as the issues. Jackie said, "Bob, I think our biggest problem is that my dad wants to have his hands in all four locations and it's just not possible. We have store managers, but they are not managing their store as much as they are selling. We don't have consistency between the stores on how we do things, other than the accounting."

I agreed with Jackie that the biggest issue was probably Matt, not because he couldn't run a store, but because he couldn't run all four stores well at the same time. Matt, like many dealers, had a hard time letting go and letting the people he hired do the jobs they were being paid to do. As we continued our conversation, I knew that Matt needed an intervention and Jackie couldn't be the one to do it.

In six weeks, we were going to be in Pennsylvania for one of our one-day management boot camps, and I encouraged Jackie to find a way to get her dad and their store managers to attend. I felt that if I had an opportunity to meet Matt on neutral ground, and if he would be open to what we had to say about processes, people, and profits, Jackie might have a chance of getting him to open up to a different way of running his dealerships.

Six weeks later in Lancaster, Pennsylvania, I had a chance to meet Matt, Jackie, and their store managers. We briefly connected at the first break, and later, I grabbed lunch with them. Matt was a sharp businessman with a great sense of humor. His managers were impressive, and Jackie was equally impressive and smart, just as I thought she would be. That day began a journey.

After the meeting in Lancaster, Matt was given the opportunity from one of his manufacturers to join one of our dealer programs. By participating, he would gain training for his people and it would help him maintain his Dealer Excellence Score with the manufacturer. During our first meeting, I, along with my team, had the opportunity to get to know Matt, Jackie, and their store managers better. Of the four managers, three had been department managers in other dealerships before working for Matt and one had been a top salesperson for a competing dealership.

None of the managers had any formal management training, and only one understood how to read a financial statement. While Matt understood his numbers, it was Jackie who knew them best of all. Matt and the team had a lot of work ahead of them, but I had no doubt that we would get them to the place where they would know their numbers, understand what they meant, and work toward improving them.

Over the next two years, week by week, month by month I watched them grow and improve. Not just the store managers, but Matt and Jackie as well. Their dealerships were on the move. I worked with Jackie using our financial trending tool to take the last five years of income statements by store, and by month, and input the numbers in service, parts, sales, and rental. This would help us build a yearly forecasting tool so each store would have an accurate budget and projections they would work to hit each month.

In the beginning, Matt was a little concerned about letting out too much of the financial information to the individual stores, but both Jackie and I encouraged him to embrace open book management for his store managers and to then allow them to do the same with their department managers for their locations.

That became the tipping point for the stores. Each manager now knew their numbers as well as the other store managers' numbers. On the first week of each new month, I meet with Matt, Jackie, their new accountant, and the store managers. They each go over their sales projections and their actuals for each department, the recovery and efficiency rates for their shop, gross profit in parts, sales, and rental, as well as their margins.

While each store is different in size, from a profit standpoint, each manager is waiting to see who has the best margins in parts, sales, and rental; what shop has the best recovery rate; and which tech, in all the stores, is the most efficient. It has become a friendly competition that lets everyone, including Matt, win.

As I look back over the last couple of years and think about my first meeting with Matt's team in Lancaster, I am really proud of each one of them and how far they have come. Not only have they grown in their understanding of the numbers they are accountable to, in addition the attitudes of the people in the dealerships have completely changed.

Part of that came from getting rid of bad hires, not bad people. Before we started, the store managers would have a hole to fill and hire a body to fill it. Now that Jackie is working with them, each job has a job description, a model of the required skill set, and the personality characteristics needed to fill the position. She has also put the correct training in place so that once a new person comes on, they can begin a training process and are not left to figure things out on their own.

While it took some time in the beginning to put it all in place, it radically reduced turnover. We have even "saved" a couple of good employees who were performing poorly in their position, by moving them to a position that fit their personality and skill set better. Rather than lose them and having to hire new people, they are thriving and enjoying their new position.

All of the stores have embraced our "hire low and grow" strategy for people. They are always growing their next "A" tech; their next service, parts, sale, and rental manager; and their next top-producing salesperson. If the dealerships have a higher-end position open in their stores, they can now fill it internally and look to replace a lower position from the outside. As Matt is looking to add more locations in the future, we have a team of highly trained people who can fill those new slots and continue the growth.

Matt and I meet briefly every week on a webcast. I shared with him that I would like to use their story in our book and asked him first if he would mind. He shared with me that every dealership should be aware of his journey and the impact it has had on him and his people. When I asked him to share the one thing that he felt was most important for other dealers to understand, regardless of the size of the dealership or the number of people they had, without pause he said, "Bob, tell dealers they need to be transparent with their people. Don't be afraid to share numbers, goals, and dreams with them. I am 100 percent convinced that is how you keep good people and grow profitable dealerships."

GROW AND DEVELOP YOUR EMPLOYEES

As Bob shared the story about Matt, I hope you noticed that to grow his dealerships, Matt first needed to understand what his goals were for his employees, and then to be open enough to sharing that information with them.

Do you know what your ultimate goal should be? Your goal is to develop and grow your employees so that, eventually, your job becomes obsolete.

Many jobs that were once necessary are now obsolete. Think about the people who used to put up pins in the bowling alley. Gone. Telephone operators are needed no more. Clowns? Unfortunately, they still exist, but their jobs should be obsolete. Seriously, they are just creepy.

Just because the job doesn't exist doesn't mean these people don't have a different job. Like you, their job has evolved and changed, and I want you to think about what that evolution looks like for you.

Think about it this way. What's the purpose of your employees if not to take things off your plate and make your dealership more money? Now, you may have one of a wide array of reactions to this. One group may be like, "Bring it on! I've been needing a break for the last thirty years." While another group may have a minor panic attack at the idea of their job becoming obsolete. There is also a group in the middle that is excited about the possibility and is willing to put in the work. This is the group that I'm most excited about because they realize there is no "easy" button, no magic wand, and no unicorns prancing through the field that causes this to happen. But, putting in the hard and consistent work now will make their job obsolete in the future. For you, maybe this means retiring while the business still generates income for you. For others, it might be a role change, where you move from being involved in every little thing that happens in the dealership to managing the business from a thirty-thousand-foot view with a focus on your numbers, your people, and training.

This last habit fully focuses on your people. Here is what I know to be true: as we have worked alongside some of the most successful dealerships across North America and beyond, they all exhibit Habits One through Six, and those habits are magnified by their people. If you don't have the first six habits in place, you will continually struggle to find, keep, and retain good people. Let that soak in for a second. I'll repeat: If you don't have the first six habits in place, you will continually struggle to find, keep, and retain good people. Sure, you may have a few employees who will be loyal to you until the end, but most of the time, if you do not have a solid base of habits in place, you will lose your good employees who are sick of the chaos, complacency, and constant frustration and will make the decision to move onto the next thing. Let's be honest, can you blame them?

At the beginning of this book, we talked about the three most important things you can do in your dealership. Do you remember them? Just in case you need a quick refresher, let me remind you. As an owner, you are responsible for: 1) creating and sharing the vision for your dealership, 2) putting together a strategy on how to get there, and 3) developing your people. Habit Seven is all about developing your people, an important part of your job. If you manage people, any people at all, it's part of your job. Maybe you just opened your dealership, and you are the only employee. It's part of your job to develop yourself. It comes down to the fact that you are responsible for not only your own growth and development but the growth and development of your employees as well. If something is over your head, either attend a class on it or reach out to others in the industry, and encourage your people to do the same. Maybe there are skills that you, or your people, are already good at but, with work, you can become an expert. The energy you put into developing yourself and your people will never go to waste.

Consistently I witness really good employees leaving dealerships because there isn't a path to grow. This doesn't necessarily mean they are working toward a management position or have a desire to run the dealership, but every person has a basic instinct to learn and be challenged, and when that stops happening, they leave. As an owner or manager, it's your job to find ways to provide opportunities for your people. Go out of your way to make them the best they possibly can be. Find and develop their skills and provide tools that make them invaluable to the dealership. In those moments, where you are going out of your way to develop your people, you are creating loyalty.

I hear it all the time: "People aren't loyal anymore." Whenever I hear that I always ask the person who says it, "When's the last time you did something to earn your people's loyalty?" The response nine times out of ten is, "Well, I give them a paycheck." That is not how you develop loyalty. If you are struggling with employee loyalty, look in the mirror and ask yourself, "Why should my employees be loyal to me?"

WHERE DO I FIND GOOD PEOPLE?

When we start talking about the people on our team, it's not uncommon to get the question "Where do we find these hypothetical good people at?" My response is always the same. There are a lot of good people looking for jobs, but maybe they just don't want to work for you. Is that harsh? Yes, a little bit. But, it's true.

Most good people aren't unemployed. I'm not saying that you should steal other people's employees, but keep in mind that if you want to attract quality candidates, you have to make your dealership attractive to those people. This doesn't stop at making sure the dealership is clean and everyone is on their best behavior when they come in for an interview. Good people will see right through the smoke screen you are putting up, just like you walking into a multilevel marketing presentation. Here are a few important notes to remember when looking to attract good people to your business.

- Good people aren't cheap.

You are not going to get a great employee for minimum wage. If your focus is on getting a great employee (which it should be, unless you want to continue to torture yourself), you are going to have to pay them for what they bring to the table. I don't care where you are; you are not going to get a quality technician with a good attitude who can turn out work for $15/hour.

- Good people aren't going to quietly do only what they are told, in the way you want it done, and leave at the end of the day.

Good people are going to challenge you and ask you why you do things the way you do. This is not because they disrespect you or question whether or not you know what you're talking about; they simply want to understand. The moment you become defensive with this type of employee, you start pushing them out the door. Now, this doesn't mean they get to be drama queens who act like they actually have a degree in rocket science and know everything there is to know, but what it does mean is that the questions they are asking can make you better. Leave your ego at the door.

- Good people are not okay with working at a place that is going nowhere.

If you are okay with the status quo, you won't find or retain good people. For you to keep good people, you have to be striving toward something they can buy into and be a part of. Many times, complacency is the reason they were looking for a new job in the first place. Don't let complacency in your dealership be part of the reason they start looking to leave your dealership as well.

HIRE LOW AND GROW

While there is an endless number of places you can find experienced employees, the best place to look is inside your dealership. We always strive to "hire low and grow" people. What this means, at its simplest form, is that you should hire people in an entry-level position and grow them into who you need them to be.

Two specific positions that work well with the "hire low and grow" mentality are the service coordinator position and the parts support specialist position.

The service coordinator is a person in the service department who helps you increase efficiency. This person is responsible for a number of items, including cleaning units before they are brought in for service, loading and unloading units, and lending a hand to the technicians as they are triaging and working on the units they service. We often say they are like a busboy or busgirl at a restaurant, getting all the tables ready for the servers to take care of the customers and move the next set of customers in.

Again, this is a low-level person we want to grow. What we see is that while they are giving technicians a hand with repairs, what is actually happening is that they are learning to become technicians themselves. When it's time for us to hire another "B" level technician, we don't have to look far because we have been training our next technician from within the whole time. It's much easier to find a service coordinator than it is to find a technician. So, once they are a technician, we would simply start this process again.

One other note on the service coordinator: if we were staffing a service department from the ground up, this is the second person we would hire. Your goal is to make them cost neutral to the dealership, and we do this by building their cost into the flat rates.

The other position we typically "hire low and grow" is a parts support specialist. This is someone you would typically hire part-time. Their role is to manage, put away, and keep track of your stocking parts orders. You know the one that sits on your floor and you step over time after time like some sort of night club dance? The one your technicians walk up to and pull the parts out of that they need and then forget to bill the customers for? This is the parts support specialist's main focus.

We typically find a parent who would like to work while their kids are in school. Typically, dealers set their hours to fit the school day, with 10:00-3:00 being the most common.

The parts support specialist spends their day learning all about parts and probably becomes more familiar with your parts inventory than anyone else. Do you know what type of knowledge you would want a parts person to have if you were to hire one? A strong familiarity with parts. Your parts support specialist touches and puts away every part that comes in your store, tags and counts them, and records them into inventory. So, when all of the stars align and your parts support specialist comes to you and asks if there is any way they could move into a full-time position as their kids get older, try to refrain from jumping up and down with excitement and say, in a calm voice, "Absolutely." Because becoming a parts person is exactly what we have been training them to do.

What do we do when we move this person to the new position? We hire another person to take their old position and start the process over again.

Hiring low and growing takes time, but it allows us to have our own feeding pool of new employees and helps us create the loyalty we are striving for.

EMPLOYEE EFFECTIVENESS RATING

One tool that we encourage all of our dealers to use twice a year is called the employee effectiveness rating (EER). We created this tool to help dealers see if they could salvage a problem employee before they, and the situation, were too far gone. It has helped thousands of dealers around the world do just that. You can print off a paper copy at bobclements.com/resources, or find a template in the appendix. This process only takes a few minutes but will give you a world of insight into your people, where you might encounter danger zones, and how you can help your people grow.

There are a few things to keep in mind. First, if you run the dealership with someone else, complete the EER separately and then share your thoughts with each other. It's interesting to see how differently others may be perceiving the people on your team. Second, if you have over twenty employees complete the

EER form for only the employees you manage directly. If you have under twenty, complete the form for everyone on your team. Third, if your spouse works in the dealership, don't be stupid by giving them low ratings! This is not something to go to marriage counseling over.

Once you print out the paper, write down the names of all the employees you oversee in the left-hand column, including yourself. Then, give them each a rating. We are going to rate them in two areas: their motivation and their competence or skill level to perform the job.

Write a (1) and give a rating of 50 percent to anyone who is **Motivated with Low Competence.**

This is someone who comes into the dealership excited and willing to do whatever is needed to do the job well or at all, but they don't have the skills needed to do the job. Many times, this is a person who is a new hire. The issue comes when this person doesn't move past the low-competence stage.

Your key focus with any employee in this stage is skills training. If you want to move them to the next place of effectiveness, they have to develop the skills needed to become competent in their job or task. We want to safeguard their motivation, by keeping them away from the people who will suck their energy and motivation while focusing on training. This is a training issue. Come up with a training plan for them.

Write a two (2) and give a rating of 75 percent to anyone who is **Motivated and Competent.**

Next, identify anyone who is motivated and has the skills to do their job. This may look like someone at the parts counter who has a good attitude, interacts with customers well, but still needs help when it comes to planning fast-moving parts placement. We aren't holding anything against this person, but we do know we need to find a way to continue to train and develop them.

Like our motivated employees with low competence, you want to safeguard them from the negative people in your dealership and identify the specific areas where they need training. You need to move them to a place of high competence, which is equivalent to mastery of the skill or the job. But the only way to get there is with specific skill training. Some of that may come from just doing the job, but we can accelerate this process by helping them identify the skills they need and giving them training for the skills.

Write a three (3) and give a rating of 100 percent to anyone who is **Motivated and Highly Competent.**

Our next group is the gold standard of employees. In an ideal world, this is where you are trying to move all of your employees. This is a place of motivation and mastery in their job. Could you imagine having a group of people who are highly motivated and have all the skills they need for their job? They do exist! If you have any employees in this category, put a three next to their name.

You need to keep in mind, with this employee, that you cannot become complacent with them. You can't just be okay with the fact that they are motivated, and trust them to count the cash drawer, open and close the dealership, and perform all of the other aspects that come with having a high trust level. You need to keep pushing and challenging them to be better and learn new skills.

These are the people, of all your people, you don't want to lose. My guess is you spent a lot of time and money to get these people to this level, so guard them like your life depends on it. The easiest way to safeguard them? Don't stop investing in ways they can get better, take on new responsibility, and be challenged.

A person who is motivated and highly competent in their skills could find a new job tomorrow somewhere else, and they know that. Guard this person and allow them to thrive within your dealership.

Write a four (4) and give a rating of 80 percent to anyone who is **Unmotivated and Highly Competent.**

This group is for employees who have the mastery of skills but don't have the excitement or willingness to do "whatever it takes" to get the job done. This is an interesting group for a number of reasons. First, there was a time when they were motivated, but something happened to move them to a place where they now have a lack of motivation. The other thing we see is that many times you, as an owner or manager, can easily slide into this category. There is probably no one in your dealership who can rival your skill set or knowledge, but, for some reason or set of reasons, you aren't motivated anymore. That fire in your belly is gone. That desire to come into the dealership and go above and beyond is no longer there. Hopefully, as you have identified your vision and strategy, it has helped reignite the fire that was once there.

One thing I know to be true in my own life is that if I don't have something big I'm striving for, it can all seem meaningless. Your people need you to re-find your motivation. If you can't find it, fake it until you do. Now, I'm not saying that you should be unauthentic; you need to be authentic with your people. However, I know if you can fake some level of excitement and enthusiasm each day, you will eventually start getting excited again, and that's what you need.

Now, if you have an employee who is in this place, you need to do the same thing with them. Help them get re-excited. What is it that stirs their soul? Is it understanding how your customers are using the product to make their life better? Share that with them. Is it researching products or ways to fix them? Let them research! We want to move this valuable person back to a place of being excited, but it starts with you moving to a place of being excited about your business again.

Write a five (5) and give a rating of 50 percent to anyone who is **Unmotivated and Competent.**

If we have an employee who is in the unmotivated but competent category, I want you to understand they aren't a lost cause. This is someone who has adequate skills but doesn't have the drive or excitement around your dealership they once did. Like I mentioned earlier, you have to help them re-find their motivation. The good news? They were motivated to be a part of your team at some point, or you wouldn't have hired them. If you had someone walk into an interview and say, "I don't like you, your dealership, or the products you sell," I can say with confidence you would not have hired them. If they are a person worth keeping, you have to move them back to a place of motivation.

The other area you need to focus on is their training. Now, I will say, if I were in your shoes, I wouldn't spend a lot of money on training them until we figure out the motivation issue. But I would spend a little money and time to see if that is one of the things that would help them move toward improving their motivation. It's expensive to find and hire new employees, so the best-case scenario is that we keep the ones we have and help them move to a place of motivation and high competence.

Write a six (6) and give a rating of 20 percent to anyone who is **Unmotivated with Low Competence.**

This is someone who probably doesn't have a long-term future with your dealership. Typically, this person shows up late and leaves early. When they are there, they do the absolute minimum required to keep their job, which means that you, or others, repeatedly have to go back and fix the problems they create.

Many times, this person has been with the dealership for a long time and is either family or has become like family. I get that this is a hard decision. But you must face the facts. First, they are sucking up valuable payroll. Second, they are a drain on every single person around them. How would it change the dynamic in your dealership if you could replace them with a motivated, competent employee?

Ultimately, how you handle this is up to you. We can't and won't force you to do anything. However, my guess is that before you got to this point of the rating, you already knew this person would be at the bottom.

Keep in mind, you can't change this person. The only person you have the ability to change is yourself. You can't change other people; that's up to them. But you can decide if you want them sucking the energy out of you, your people, your business, and your customers (just say no to vampires in your dealership). Ultimately, you get to decide whether or not you want to work with energy vampires every day.

Now that you have walked through everyone on your team, I want you to put a percentage rating in the third column and add it up. Don't do this in your head. You don't need to prove anything to me. Get your calculator out.

Take the total of all of your employees and then divide the total number by the numbers of employees you have. What's your number? My challenge to you is to increase the number by 10 percent over the next six months. Will this take time and work? Yes. But most things that are worth doing, in the long run, are never really easy.

THE RIGHT PEOPLE, IN THE RIGHT POSITION IN YOUR DEALERSHIP, IS ONE OF YOUR GREATEST ASSETS

We were working with a dealer who was in a hard place with one of his employees. He had hired a young woman to work in the service department as a service writer, but for some reason she just wasn't a fit. He couldn't understand where the disconnect was. She was enthusiastic, loved helping customers, had an eye for detail, and enjoyed the industry. As much as the owner tried willing her to succeed in the service writer position, it became clear over and over that she wasn't the right fit.

As this owner was working with our team, we kept coming back to this young woman and her potential for the dealership, but there was something off.

This owner decided to take a leap of faith and move this young, energetic woman to the parts counter. She had a basic understanding of parts, from her work in the service department, and her customer-first attitude was contagious. This move from the service department to the parts department was exactly the right move. This young woman took on her new position with new-found enthusiasm, allowing her to do all of the things she excelled at and thrived.

The biggest impact wasn't just on her and her potential, but the impact she had on the rest of the parts department staff. She brought a new excitement and energy that raised the bar for everyone at the parts department, and she is thriving in her new position.

Sometimes, the issue with people is not actually about the people. Maybe you have put them in the wrong position. If this is the case, you have set them up for failure. You have to make sure that your people are in the right spots to thrive.

To be clear, having the right people in the right place doesn't mean that everyone on your team only does things that "spark joy." Oh please, that's not how this works. Instead, if you can have your people in a place where they are enjoying their job and working to their strengths the majority of the time, both you and they are winning. Then you will have motivated and engaged employees who strive to make your dealership part of their long-term plan. This is what you are striving for.

Have you ever been part of a sport or an activity that you were terrible at? My guess is probably. For me, it wasn't just one sport; it ran the gamut: soccer, ice skating, basketball, tennis . . . the list goes on. Basically, any skill that required me to have any coordination I failed miserably at. One year, in fifth grade, I told my mom I wanted to play soccer and she signed me up. Honestly, if she would have loved me she would have looked me in the eyes and said, "Sara, you are terrible at soccer, this isn't going to go well." But, she didn't. As soon as I finished my first practice (you know, the one where you basically introduce yourself and kick the ball three times), I knew this was going to be bad. I told my mom that night I wanted to quit, and she pulled a "Sara, you made a commitment to your team, you are going to do this and have a good attitude." Don't you hate it when your parents raise you to be decent human beings?

So, I went to practice, and it became more and more obvious that I was in fact terrible at soccer, like, scoring-a-goal-for-the-other-team terrible. I followed through on my commitment and spent most of my fifth-grade soccer season sitting on the bench. (Don't feel bad for me. Everyone won in this situation.)

Here is the thing. It's easy to put a good person in the wrong position and set them up to fail. You don't ever mean to, but you had a spot to fill and they seemed like they would do a fine job. So out of necessity you put them in the position, but it never becomes a great fit. Thankfully, though, you have the ability to change this and find the right position for them.

We see this over and over again in dealerships. You think you're giving someone the opportunity to "move up the ladder" and you're really setting them up to fail. One position we see this, more than any other, is when a dealer moves their best technician into the role of the service manager. In most cases, this is a terrible idea. Think about it. Your best technicians are the best because they like to figure out how to fix a problem. It's not because they love dealing with people. But what is required of a service manager? Dealing with a lot of people. And now you have taken one of your top revenue producers and put them in a place where they are not actively generating revenue for your service department, and they hate what they are doing. You have set them up to fail.

What I do know is that something incredible happens when you have the right people in the right spots. They are motivated and they work to improve their skills, on their own. You no longer have to pull them along and feel like you are doing all of the work to encourage them to get better; they strive for that on their own. It doesn't happen overnight, but when you have the right people in the right place you will see an entirely different side of passion and motivation coming from them.

TRANSPARENCY WITH YOUR PEOPLE

The idea of becoming transparent with your employees is something that sends most dealers into a level of stress that is equivalent of finding out your firstborn is a Teenage Mutant Ninja Turtle.

When we talk to dealers about transparency, we typically get a string of objections, but here are the ones we hear most frequently:

- What happens if I am transparent and they use the information against me?
- What if they figure out that I have no idea what I'm talking about?
- What if they know entirely too much?

My thought is, what if the opposite is true?

- What if they take the information you shared and use it to better your business?
- What if you have the opportunity to learn together?
- What if they know enough to do their job more effectively?

The direction you go is up to you!

. . .

Remember when Matt began to bring his managers together to meet? He began by just using the basic numbers that we reviewed in Habit Four. Using his Dealer Management Software, each store and department is able to pull a few of their key performance indicators (numbers) regarding sales of whole goods and parts as well as service performance. As soon as they begin to see any downturn or possible problem, they visit about what they can do to change course.

The point is you don't have to start big; start small. Begin to pull, track regularly, and talk about one or two key performance indicators in each department. Work to understand what that number means and how you can improve it. By starting small and meeting consistently with your key employees, you will begin to increase your comfort in sharing information that will help them do their jobs better. Baby steps, but just keep walking.

Let's be clear about one thing when it comes to transparency. Transparency with your people doesn't mean that every single person in your dealership gets the privilege of knowing all of the information about your dealership.

I don't expect you to share your profit-and-loss statement with all of your employees, nor would I recommend it. What I do want you to do is ask yourself the question, "Who can I bring into the conversation?"

Transparency in your dealership is one of the ways to develop your people and to eventually make your job obsolete. You won't be able to work yourself out of the business if no one in your dealership knows how to look at the numbers and make decisions based on them. This requires transparency. So, how do you do this?

What happens if I am transparent and they use the information against me?

Decide who you are going to bring into the fold, and what information you want to share with them.

You know your people, and you know who can handle the information you are going to share. I encourage you to use your Employee Effectiveness Rating as a guide and start with the people who are the motivated, highly competent employees.

The conversation with this group could be around specific numbers by department, or even things like salary caps, or profit and loss. It's up to you to decide what and how much you want to share. Will this be scary at first? Yes. Will you get it wrong along the way and share too much or too little? Probably. But transparency involves more than just sharing the numbers and status of your dealership; it also involves you being open to learning how to do this alongside your people.

Maybe your whole team needs a wake-up call on a high level of what it really takes to keep the dealership running. A few years ago, I saw a video online that outlined how one business owner did just that. He wanted to show his people just what was left at the end of the day for him to receive any profit (since his people assumed that he had a swimming pool full of hundred-dollar bills at his house).

Here is what he did. He got a million dollars' worth of Monopoly money and laid it out on a table. His people oohed and awed at the money, thinking that all of their preconceived notions were right, and he was just selfish. He then removed the money he needed to pay for rent, utilities, and other fixed expenses in the dealership. The pile of money started to dwindle.

Then, he removed the money that he used for payroll, each year, out of the mix, followed by his cost of goods sold and so on until there was just a very small amount of Monopoly money left on the table. His team finally had the revelation of what the actual financial commitment was to run the business, and the owner was able to be transparent with his entire team without sharing specific numbers.

I will say, each department should know the state of their department. This is something that the department manager, if you have one, should communicate regularly with their team. We typically tie employee bonuses into each department's profitability. So, if you take this stance, your people will have a vested interest in knowing the numbers.

What if they figure out that I have no idea what I'm talking about?

Ah, our egos always get in the way of progress. My guess is if this is your fear, first, you probably know more than what you are giving yourself credit for, and second, your people have the same fear.

Are there a lot of things you don't know about in your business? My guess is yes. Like I said before, most of you didn't start your dealership because you couldn't wait to dive into the financials or marketing or HR side of the business. No, most of you started it because you loved the product you were going to sell, or enjoyed fixing things or even found that interacting with customers was fun.

The truth is that the people you are working to be transparent with probably didn't join your team because they loved those things either. You taking the steps to learn and grow will only encourage them to learn and grow along with you.

What if they know entirely too much?

Inside of our company, we try to lean on the side of giving too much information versus too little. We know that we have a good team, made up of individuals who are all trying to do the same thing—move our business forward—and to do that they need as much information as possible to help them achieve that.

Do we always get it right? No. Do we try again and again? Yes. When we can give our people the information they need in order to move our business forward, we are in a place that allows our people to push the envelope, as long as it stays within our mission, vision, and core values.

Keep in mind, if we were in your shoes, we would also have our employees sign confidentiality agreements and non-competes when we are hiring. We do know that our people will have access to information that is sensitive. Even the employees who don't have access to the details of the company financials will have other information on the processes and procedures of your business, so safeguard yourself and make sure you are covered from the beginning.

WOULD YOU WANT TO WORK AT YOUR DEALERSHIP?

At this point, I feel like you and I are friends. I'm confident throughout this book, I've probably insulted you, told you all about many of my flaws (don't worry, there are more), and shared stories about my kids and our own crazy family business; so in my mind, that means we are friends.

As a friend, I'm going to ask you this and I want you to be honest, friend to friend. As your dealership sits right now, would you want to work there as an employee? While we are book friends now, I won't ever know your answer unless you come up to me after an event and tell me. If the answer is "Yes," I'm pumped for you. I know there has been a lot of hard work to get to that point, and I'm proud of you. If the answer is "Not yet," I want to remind you that you have been given the resources to change the future of your dealership, if you make the decision to implement them. Regardless of where you are, one final part of using your people comes down to fun. It's up to you, as the owner and manager, to make the dealership a fun place to work. So, let's talk about fun.

Making your dealership fun doesn't have to be complex. It might be a break room stocked with snacks and sodas that your employees can get as they need throughout the day. One dealer we work with buys lunch for his team twice a week from a local restaurant in his community, and his people love it. It could even be as simple as contests where your people have to guess the number of nuts and washers in a jar and the person who gets closest wins a gift card to a local restaurant. I don't know what it is specifically for your dealership, but I do know that doing small, fun, and unexpected things helps to create an enjoyable environment for everyone.

Do you know what the top two things are that keep people from leaving their current job? Despite what you may think, it's not money. It's the connection they have with their co-workers along with feeling as though they are a part of something that matters.

We work with one dealer who really knows how to build a cohesive workforce, the type of team that really enjoys being together. How do I know? Because their employees were willing to all load into an RV and travel over five hundred miles to attend a training event together. Now, you don't get into an RV for a ten-hour road trip with people you don't like.

You, as the owner or manager, must focus on going the extra mile to make your dealership a place your people enjoy working. Meet with your people individually. Have your people meet as a team. Incorporate some fun into the daily routine. Perhaps include their families in quarterly events such as a picnic or barbecue.

You hire them, train them, develop them, and pay them. They work hard for you, improve your business, and take good care of your customers. Make the effort to create a cohesive team. You will be glad you did, and maybe you will move to a place where being at the dealership is even fun for you, and if I were to ask you if you wanted to work there, as a friend, you would say "Yes!"

Inside of a dealership, there are many aspects that signify your health, but your people are one of the greatest assets to your business. At the end of the day your people are simply a magnifier to whatever is already happening inside the walls of your dealership. If you are in an endless cycle of struggle, where you never feel like you can get ahead, you will struggle with turnover and the people you do have will magnify that. If you have made the decision to take back control of your sanity, your life, and your dealership by implementing these seven habits, your people will magnify that as well. It's up to you to decide what kind of base you are building for your dealership and then allow your people to magnify it, because you, my friend, are the solution.

Conclusion

I think that Sara would agree with me when I say we are all on a wonderful journey called life. While it is not always an easy journey, it is always an interesting one. I grew up on a farm near a small little town in the northwest corner of Missouri. Never in my wildest dreams could I have imagined the places I would end up traveling to around the world or the people I would have the privilege of meeting along the way. Each person I have met along my journey has added to my knowledge and helped me and my team offer guidance, direction, and hope to thousands of dealers across the country.

The goal Sara and I had in writing this book was to give encouragement and hope to dealers who are struggling, and for those who are succeeding in business, a positive and helpful reminder that you are doing great! While your situation might be slightly different than the dealers highlighted in the seven habits, we believe that every dealer who reads this book will find a little bit of themselves and their situations in the stories we shared. We also hope that whatever battle you are facing, you are realizing that just as these dealers were able to overcome their hurdles, so can you.

While I did change the locations and names of the people in the stories I shared with you, I did not change the situations they were in nor the outcome they had. I would like to take a moment to reintroduce you to these dealers and share with you where their journey has taken them.

Having a clear vision for the future was the first habit Sara shared with you. I introduced you to the young couple that I connected with at the GIE+EXPO in Louisville, Kentucky. Ron and Marsha were working themselves into the ground.

They were tired, frustrated, and had lost their passion for the business. But the problem was not really that they had lost their passion, but they had forgotten why they had started the dealership in the first place. When they began, their vision for the dealership was to allow them the freedom to go anywhere they wanted to go and do anything they wanted to do. They were so caught up in the business, and allowed themselves to be pulled in any direction the wind blew, that they were failing to run the business. I was able to help them refocus their energies on why they started the business in the first place. Through the process they began to reignite their passion and excitement.

I am honored to have worked with them both and excited to share that they are no longer a slave to the business. They have built a wonderful team and now own a second home in the beautiful state of Florida on the Gulf Coast where they spend about half of each year.

Ron and Marsha, you know who you are. I am proud to call you both friends and to have been able to be a part of your journey.

If you remember, ***change*** was the focus of Habit Two. In this chapter I introduced you to two dealers. The first was Rachel and her son Jason. Rachel's husband decided to start a dealership when they were first married, and she worked to support him to the best of her ability. They had a son, Jason, and over the years Rachel saw her husband spending more and more time and making less and less money.

Unfortunately, they decided to separate. As Rachel was watching her son Jason follow in the footsteps of his dad, she made the decision to pay for him to attend one of our management boot camps. During the meeting, I was so impressed with the passion that Jason had for learning, I offered to have my team work with him for free as a part of our Dealer Success Groups. He simply had to be willing to make the changes we recommended and be open to learning how to run the dealership in a different way. He took us up on the offer, and after working through some battles with his dad over the next twelve months began transforming their business.

I never had the opportunity to meet Rachel again after that day in Tacoma, but Jason is still working with us in the program. Jason and his dad have a dealership now that is growing stronger and more profitable by the year. Jason's dad now takes time off, and the last I knew he was working on building a cabin on a piece of property he had owned for years always hoping someday to be able to retire from the business and have his son carry it on.

Because Jason did what we asked him to do, even though at times it was very uncomfortable, combined with his desire to constantly learn, Jason and his family have a bright future ahead of them. That's right, I forgot to mention that Jason is soon to be a father for the first time! Congratulations!

One last note to Rachel: Jason is blessed to have you as his mother. Your love and concern for his future, and the action you took on his behalf, has changed his life forever. I hope someday to meet you again.

I also introduced to you, as a part of chapter 2, **the habit of change**, to Kathy who came back to work in a dealership to help her dad and mom, Keith and Virginia, rebrand and transform their fifty-year-old business. The one manufacturer they had built their business around for over five decades made a decision not to renew their agreement, and instead gave their line to another dealership who had multiple locations. And, for the record, I am not knocking the manufacturer; they had a perfect right to do that as a part of their business strategy. And it did not have a long-term, negative impact on Keith, Virginia, and Kathy.

Kathy, Keith, and Virginia were ready to move the dealership in a new direction but were struggling to get their people on board. Actually, they ended up having one person, a toxic parts manager, who was sabotaging their efforts and trying to infect everyone else in the dealership with his poison. As you remember, the parts manager ended up finding another dealership to work at after Kathy, Keith, and Virginia changed their strategy with him. Instead of getting pulled into his toxicity, they gave him an option of changing his attitude or changing to another company. He ended up leaving, they moved one of his parts people to department manager, and everyone in the dealership was excited again.

While the change they made was just one person, the impact on the dealership was immeasurable. Was it a difficult change to make? It was at the time, but I think Kathy and her parents would say that if they ever have to face a situation like that again, it will be easier and they wouldn't wait nearly as long to do it.

So how are Kathy, Keith, Virginia, and their dealership doing today? Great! While they still have some uphill battles to fight after losing such an important part of their business, they have realigned their products to attract more of the baby boomers who have the money to purchase their equipment and the organic farmers in their area who are looking for both knowledge and equipment to help them be profitable. I am excited to say that I meet with Kathy, Keith, and their management team once a week, and I fully expect them to have success. Kathy, thanks for making that first phone call to me. Keith and Virginia, thanks for believing in your daughter, for your willingness to be open to new ideas, and for your friendship.

Habit Three focused on **understanding and applying the resources** that are available to you and your dealership. You met Justin and Abby who asked me what piece of advice I would give them as they were taking over the family business. In that same story I also introduced you to Scott. I shared his story, and if you remember, he had a partner who died. Scott had multiple years of dry weather, a financial crisis, and a top salesperson who left and went to a competitor. In each situation Scott would look at the resources he had available and would use those, along with the knowledge he gained, to lead him through each challenge. From the manufacturers, associations, banker, accountant, outside consulting, and even his people, Scott was able to move forward. He would tell you the key to his success is his willingness to leave his ego and pride at the door. To ask for and then be willing to accept the help that others make available to you. That was the one piece of advice that I gave to Justin and Abby as they went on their journey to take over the family business. I am excited to say that Scott's dealership is going as strong as ever and that Justin and Abby did take over the business. They are having a great time and are looking to add a second location in the near future. Thanks to you all for allowing me to share your stories!

Knowing and understanding your numbers was Habit Four. Here, I introduced you to a father and son team, Ron and Kyle. Their challenge was not so much how to make money, but how to actually keep it. While they had software they were running in their business, neither Ron nor Kyle had really taken the time to understand all the reporting it was able to give them. Each month they would look at the bottom line on their profit-and-loss statement, and if it showed they were profitable, that was good enough. In working with them both, my team helped them recognize their key performance numbers in each department and showed them how to make improvements on them. They found that the reports help them improve not only their profits but also their employees' performance. We worked with Ron and Kyle to create performance-based compensation programs so that as the business generated more profit, the employees benefited as well. Ron and Kyle's ultimate goal is to eliminate floor planning and pay for their units with cash. They adopted the profit-first approach that Sara shared with you and are well on their way. Ron and Kyle have a strong, bright future ahead of them and I am honored that they allowed me to share part of their journey with you.

In Habit Five, Sara focused on the importance of **attitude and action.** This is one of the traits that I see in so many successful dealers. In the beginning of the chapter I introduced you to Michael. We had met years ago and had become great friends. Michael left the corporate world and took on the reins of a three-generation business.

In the process, Michael took on a partner and between the two of them grew from a single location to a three-store operation.

Michael battled with many challenges: competitors, the economy, and employee theft. With every battle Michael kept his sense of perspective, never let his attitude falter, and continued to move forward. Michael's true test came with the news of an accident that a driver of his had left one person dead and another severely injured. It also resulted in a prison sentence for the young driver, and a massive lawsuit that Michael didn't have enough insurance to cover.

Michael pulled together the resources he had, much like Scott in our last habit, and over a period of a couple of years worked everything out. Was it probably the biggest challenge Michael had ever faced? I am sure it was. But all through the journey, Michael had great faith, kept his attitude positive, and continued to find ways to move forward.

I wanted to share Michael's story with you to reinforce that no matter what happens, with faith, the right attitude, and a willingness to never give up, you can surmount any problem that faces you. Michael, you are a great friend that I am blessed to have. I know that your story will touch many lives. Thanks for allowing me to share it.

Managing time was the focus of Habit Six. April and Dan were a young couple who had the opportunity to buy a dealership from friends of the family. As a young couple with no children, they had allowed the business to become their life. But that changed with April expecting a baby and wanting to move herself into more of a part-time role. Prior to the baby being born, I started working with them on the importance of setting boundaries in the dealership so they could establish the right balance between the business and their personal lives. While in the beginning they both struggled, they finally developed habits that have provided huge benefits for both them, their three children, and their dealership. April and Dan, I am thankful that you were open enough to go through the pain of creating those boundaries years ago. What you achieved will be a motivator for others, regardless of their age, to do the same thing. Thanks to you both!

Habit Seven focused on having **the right people on the team.** I introduced you to Jackie and Matt. Jackie was Matt's daughter. She had finished college with a business degree and was asked by Matt to join him in the business. At this point, Matt had four locations that were running him into the ground. After some behind-the-scenes work with Jackie, she convinced her dad to bring the store managers and attend one of our boot camps. While there, I had the opportunity to share with them the importance of each person being responsible for their own store, of knowing their numbers, and of Matt becoming more transparent and utilizing open book management. Through the process, the managers grew in knowledge, skills, and confidence. They now understand every number in their store and have begun working with their department managers in a transparent way that allows each of them to grow into their roles, in turn expanding the dealerships.

I am excited to report that Matt, Jackie, and their stores are doing great. Matt is looking to expand into some new equipment categories and is on the lookout for his next dealership purchase. He now has the right people in place, which gives him the ability to focus his attention on new opportunities. I still meet with Matt once a week for a brief conversation and Jackie and their managers monthly as a part of our Dealer Program. Matt and Jackie, it has been a pleasure to watch how you allow your managers to manage and your willingness to be transparent with your numbers. Thanks to you both for allowing me to share your story and inspire others.

I also want to thank you, the readers, for giving Sara and me the opportunity to share what we have learned over the last thirty-five years as we have been working with dealerships. As I mentioned, I hope that, by sharing these stories from a few of the dealers I have worked with, you might find a little of yourself and your situation in each of them.

It's important for you to understand that you are not alone. There are thousands of dealers, just like yourself, who have gone through the same battle you may be fighting at this very moment. They made it through and so can you.

We live in a country and in a time where you can make your dreams a reality. Does it take hard work? Sure it does. But my guess is that you are already putting in hard work; you just need to make sure you are focusing your effort on the things that will bring about the change you are trying to achieve.

You don't need me or anyone else to tell you what doesn't work—you already know that. If you think that working harder is the answer, it's not. The key to success is your ability to change how you think about your situation, as well as your ability to see that what you have done in the past isn't getting you to where you want to go. I always share with my dealers that it's not big, earth-shattering changes you need to make. It's all about making the right small changes that will get you to the finish line.

Many times, in my workshops, I use the example of what impact a one-degree change in temperature can have. Water at 211 degrees Fahrenheit is still water. Hot water, but still water. To transform it into something different, something more powerful, it takes just one more degree of heat. The moment water reaches a temperature of 212 degrees, it begins to transform from a liquid to a gas, from water into steam.

The same holds true with water that has a temperature of 33 degrees Fahrenheit. At 33 degrees, while it is colder than water at 211 degrees it is still just water. But by removing just 1 degree of temperature, again, a transformation begins to take place moving a liquid to a solid, water into ice.

While most of us wouldn't consider a one-degree change in temperature to be significant, it can be truly transformational. That's my challenge to you. Begin to rethink how you see things in your business. Look for opportunities to make minor changes that will create major transformational shifts in how you run your dealership.

Develop the habits that we shared with you throughout this book and make today the day you begin your journey on reclaiming your sanity, and your life, and your dealership.

APPENDIX 1

Ribbon Color Guide

RED	Equipment dropped off for repair.
BLUE	Equipment has been triaged.
GREEN	Tech has certified the equipment has been serviced/repaired and is ready for customer pickup.
RED/BLACK	Tech does not want the engine started without his permission.
YELLOW	Tech has found a problem that needs additional parts or labor. Service Writer to contact customer.
WHITE	Customer has chosen not to repair equipment.

APPENDIX 2

Reporting Metrics for Dealerships

SERVICE DEPARTMENT REPORTING

Recovery Rate by technician = Billed Hours / Paid Hours for tech—**85%+**

Recovery Rate for department = Total Billed Hours / Total Paid Hours—**75%+**

Tech Efficiency = Billed Hours / Actual time clocked on to work order—**85%+**

Completion time by tech = Completed work orders / actual time—**varies based upon unit type**

Average Completion Time for Shop = Total completed work orders / Total Actual Time—**varies based upon unit type**

Labor to Parts Ratio = Total Parts Sales Sold to Service Department / Total Labor Sales—**1 to 0.6**

PARTS DEPARTMENT REPORTING

Average Sales per Transaction = Total Parts Dollars Sold / Transactions—**varies on unit type at each dealer**

Average Transaction Per Counter Sales Person = Total Transactions / # of Counter Sales People—**varies based upon dealership type**

Average Transaction Time = Start to finish time with counter customer **7 to 15 minutes depending on unit type. No more than 15 minutes regardless.**

Fill Rate out of stocking inventory = Total Parts Sold – Lost Sales,
Special Orders and Emergency Orders / Total Parts Sold—**90%**

Gross Profit Margin by Vendor = Parts COGS / Parts Sales—
varies by dealer type

Inventory Turns = Inventory Cost of Goods Sold / Inventory

Inventory Days on Hand = 365 / Inventory Turns—
90 days at season

SALES DEPARTMENT REPORTING

Gross Profit Margin by Vendor = Wholegoods COGS / Wholegood
Sales—**varies based upon product type**

Avg Sales per Sales Person = Total Sales / # Sales people—
varies based upon product type

Closing Ratio = Quotes / Sales Transactions—**40%**

BUSINESS DEPARTMENT REPORTING

Return on Sales (Net income produced on each dollar sold) =
Total Sales – Total COGS – Operating Expenses / Total Sales—
varies based upon unit type

Operating Expenses Ratio = General Administrative Expenses / Sales—
varies based upon dealer type

Current Ratio = Current Assets / Current Liabilities—**2 to 1**

Quick Ratio = (Current Assets - Inventory) / Current Liabilities—**1 to 1**

Absorption Rate = Operating Expenses (Parts, Service, Fixed
Expenses and Dealer Salary) / Gross Profit (Parts and Service
Only)—**80%**

Account Receivable Turnover = Sales / Receivables

Account Receivable Days = 365 / Account Receivable Turnover

Account Payable Turnover = Cost of Goods Sold / Payables—
if no discount

Account Payable Days = 365 / Account Payable Turnover

APPENDIX 3

Employee Effectiveness Rating Worksheet

(See following page)

EMPLOYEE EFFECTIVENESS RATING

1. Motivated/Low Competence 50%
2. Motivated/Competent 75%
3. Motivated/Highly Competent 100%

4. Unmotivated/High Competent 80%
5. Unmotivated/Competent 50%
6. Unmotivated/Low Competence 20%

EMPLOYEE	RATING	VALUE

Total # Employees_____   Total Value_____   Value/Employees_____